You just wait until your father

Introduction

Growing up in the five valleys that surround Stroud in the 1950's, 1960's and 1970's was significantly different to growing up in present times. Stroud itself is viewed by many as being one of the best towns in the country, at the same time being very diverse. Was it the same 70+ years ago?

We know how lucky children and teenagers are today but, in a village setting with no internet, no computer, no TV, no mobile phone, no expensive toy, no car, no fast food, no electric scooter, no foreign holiday - and no central heating, what did we do? We made our own fun and did as we were told, usually. Certainly, we had respect for our elders, parents and those in authority – or else!

I have called upon the memories that I hold from that era, along with a multitude of stories, anecdotes and photos from others who had their childhood pretty much at the same time, *which are shown in italics* and interwoven within my story. My hope is of being able to conjure up a picture of what growing up in the area, and even further afield, was all about – in bygone days.

First, we go back to 1937.

"Dear Diary, October 2nd 1937. The Rover Hut was opened by Lt.Col.Walton from HQ. The Rangers made cakes and about 4.30pm the hut was opened. Mr.F.L.Daniels was presented with a Thanks Badge for all he had done for the Rovers. About 5.00pm we had tea and all the cakes sold. At 7.30pm the Rovers and Rangers gathered in the hut for a Camp Fire. We had songs and then lantern slides of camp. During the slides we met Ron Hyett and Ron Wilkins (Rovers from Gloucester). We enjoyed it very much. Afterwards we had cocoa and then Ron W. and Ron H. took us home. I arranged to meet Ron W. next day and promised to write to him. So that ended a lovely day. F.N. The weather was Perfect!"

This extract taken from the diary of Norah Davis, from Rubblehole, Kingscourt, was the opening of the Rover Hut opposite Rodborough Tabernacle and the start of a relationship that saw my mother marry Ron Wilkins and as they say, the rest is history.

Front Cover Photos: Kingscourt from the top of the postman's path, Rodborough Common, taken by my son Aaron in 2021.

Kingscourt Primary School – P.E. in the playground
(Photo: Remembering Rodborough)

Back Cover Photo: Pifco multi-colour torch, an amazing Christmas present

August 2019, and the primary school reunion in the old school playground

Cover design: Grateful to my daughter Amber in Vancouver, Canada who has designed the cover on each of my five books, this one with a leaning towards the artwork of Enid Blyton books.

ISBN 978-0-9570775-2-2

The Rover Hut nearing completion in 1937 (Photo: Jennifer Hardy (Short))

My parents' wedding in June 1942, L-R Albert & Phyllis Wilkins (grandparents) Elsie Wilkins (auntie), Eric Wilkins (uncle), dad, mum, Eunice Blandford, Joan Stafford, Frank & Fanny Davis (grandparents). I don't recognize the younger bridesmaid.

BIRTH!

June 20th 1953, not a day I remember but certainly one that my mother did! Kicking and screaming I entered the world in Gloucester Maternity Hospital, which coincidentally is where my two children Amber and Aaron were born in 1985 and 1989 respectively.

Family Christmas photo 1953

At that time my parents, and older sister Cheryl, lived in the house of my grandmother, Fanny Davis. This was 'Vermand' in Kingscourt, named as such by my late grandfather after he saw action in Vermand, Northern France in WW1. A grandfather I never knew as he died of peritonitis during WW2.

'Vermand' circa 2018, the back garden was huge! (Photo: Google Street View)

1954, safe in my mother's arms on Minchinhampton common

My very first memory would have been when I was about 3 years old or so. I found some lovely, boiled sweets in the house and proceeded to start crunching away on a few, they were not sweets but marbles! Blood came from my mouth, and my mother had a freaking fit. Dad was called home from work and I went off to Stroud Hospital. The doctor said the particle(s) would go the natural way, but if I was to start rolling in agony I was to be brought straight back. My mother apparently sat by my bedside all night, just in case. The casualty department became very familiar with me over 3 decades!

On a later occasion Ron Hyett, my father's Rover Scout friend, who had emigrated to South Africa at the end of WW2, was back in England visiting. While they all sat in the lounge drinking tea, I ventured up the garden path to the tool shed at the very top – and found an open tin of green paint. When my mother came looking for me later, she found a very green child – standing with a paint brush alongside a green string of onions, green potatoes in a tray and a green lawnmower. I also recall that was my first smack!

Not much later I had a tricycle and would ride it around the garden until one day the gate was open and out I went onto Kitesnest Lane. This was a very fast tricycle, no doubt because it had no brakes, and I sped down the hill hitting the bank and flying into the road. Blood pouring from a head wound the size of an egg, and onto Stroud Hospital casualty department again.

I had a friend in Kingscourt, Peter Cornish, who lived in the Post Office that was in Bowl Hill. We were inseparable and would venture around and out of the village whenever we had the chance. I am sure there were paedophiles even then, but no one seemed that worried. Peter Cornish and I found an old pram dumped up at Little London, so we took it back to his house. The following day we took turns pushing each other around the village and eventually further afield. Mrs. Taylor, who lived at the top of Rooksmoor Hill, received a phone call from someone in North Woodchester who had spotted us happily wheeling each other along the A46 towards Nailsworth. Mrs. Taylor was one of only a handful of local villagers who had a phone as her husband ran a building business, and she rushed first to my mother and then to Peter's mother to raise the alarm. When we eventually got 'caught' my mother uttered those immortal words that I was to hear many more times – **"You just wait until your father gets home"**. We were about 4 years old!

My grandmother, Cheryl and me around 1956

As a 4-year-old I found the neighbours each side of my grandmother's house a little weird. On one side was Miss Antill who lived with her sister or maybe it was a 'friend'. She must have been very old in my eyes, about 140 years old, but she had a lovely nature. She would put a few sweets in a paper bag and poke them through the fence when I wasn't looking. Then she would squeak in a high-pitched voice, "little mouse!" and rush back indoors. On hearing this wherever I was in the house I would run into the garden to gain my treasure.

The other side was Mr. & Mrs. Hogg; he was a builder as far as I remember. By their back door was a rotary pump fixed to the wall. Every now and then either of them would go outside and crank the pump handle left then right, I found this very amusing and always asked if I could have a go. I didn't realise that they had no water pressure so had to pump the water up into a tank in the loft. They were also quite strict, and I was a little afraid of Mr. Hogg until they invited a 4-year-old around to tea one evening. Not called 'dinner' or 'supper' in those days. Tea was at teatime; dinner was at dinner time. My grandmother told me to be on my best behaviour and to remember my 'please' and 'thank you' and off I went. I don't remember what we had, but they had a sauce bottle on the table, and I asked if I could have some. Passed to me I remembered that my father always shook the bottle vigorously before pouring so I did the same – oh my, ketchup went everywhere, Mr. Hogg went red in the face then blew a fuse, and I was sent home. I was never invited again.

Mr. Hogg teaching me to be a builder – not!

Girls were not really on the radar yet, but one that I did know well was Eira Savage who lived in the bungalow at the top of Kitesnest Lane, bang opposite my grandmother's house. Initially we would shout at each other from our gardens until finally my mother took me across the road to their bungalow to meet her properly, along with her parents and older brother Roger. Going into their spacious kitchen I saw an object that I had never seen before, they had a full-size Aga range, which completely fascinated me!

My grandmother and mother were quite religious, chapel folk at Rodborough Tabernacle, as were my uncle Arthur Davis and two aunts – Kitty Holder and Mildred Neal. Every Saturday evening without fail my uncle and his wife Louie would drive over from their house in Lower Spillman's and my aunt Kitty would walk down from her house in The Street along with her husband Joe. Dad and Joe would go off to the Kings Head for some reason, he said things like, "I'm going to see a man about a dog" or "I'm going there and back to see how far it is". We never got a dog, and he never told me the distance. Often, they would take a bag or two of fruit and veg that they grew in their huge gardens (as folk did in those days) and 'bartering' would take place down the pub and other fruit and veg was brought back to help supplement Sunday dinner.

While all this was going on I had to sit quietly in the lounge with the rest of the bunch listening to a load of boring chat, I hated it, and it went on for years. My aunt Mildred would go to Erinoids club first to play bingo and always arrive back at our place just in time for supper, she had more sense as far as I could see.

Occasionally a Saturday was a bit more fun as my father worked every Saturday morning then went to the Kings Head before lunch, and sometimes he would take me – a small bottle of pop with a cardboard waxed straw and a packet of Smiths crisps. The only flavour as far as I knew, plain with a little blue bag with salt, how healthy thinking was that salt or no salt. Years later when I was at secondary school our English teacher, 'Gandhi' Levitt, would often remark for some bizarre reason, "love crisps but don't eat the blue ones!".

Now, here is a coincidence. Rhoda Wood Truman (1824-1910) was my maternal great, great, Grandmother. She married George Barter in 1850, but he died in 1867. Rhoda took on the job of landlady of the Beer House in Kingscourt and when she was 50, she married Alfred Niblett and they lived then in the Kings Head where

Rhoda was the landlady and Alfred the landlord. Alfred died in 1892, but Rhoda continued as landlady until 1901. Rhoda had 6 children by her first husband and one by Alfred born in 1871, presumably out of wedlock!

Kings Head pictured in Edwardian times and Alfred is believed to be in this photo. The building on the far right was the outside toilets (Photo: unknown)

We didn't get electricity until 1954, so candles at bedtime; paraffin lamps hanging from the beams for knitting, sewing, reading, or playing games on the kitchen table. Daytime was spent helping the grown-ups on the farm; cuddling chickens, lambs or calves; playing in the barn loft; or roaming in the gorse and bracken on the hill. One day, I found a small Welsh pony standing next to his dead mother. The owner didn't think he would survive without his dam, so let us keep him. Our Shire mare had lost her foal a few days before, so she adopted Jack who grew to be a lovely adult. Mary Potter, Glamorgan

Albert and Mrs. Buckingham lived at the bottom of Bowl Hill, she was the cleaner at the primary school, and I presume Albert worked for the town or parish council. He would go through the village weeding the verges, clearing the gutters, hedge cutting, etc. accompanied by his horse and cart. The other strange sight in the village was the weekly appearance of the Coop mobile shop, we had no other shop in the village, and this brought much-needed supplies right to the doorstep.

Other services came to the village too. Apart from the milkman and the Coop mobile shop we had a breadman, a fishman and another man who I think was a butcher or grocer, he had an old van full of supplies too, it was a very distinctive green Morris 'J' type.

Rodborough common was our playground. During the summer holidays my cousin Rod, who lived in the cottages at the bottom of Bowl Hill, would disappear on to the common sometimes armed with 6d which at Winstone's would get us ice cream. Many days were spent there and at my nans who lived in Bowl Hill

Cottages later taken down, and they were moved into the council houses and bungalow built on Kingscourt field or what we used as our field. We found bushes which had hollowed out insides. Hitching a ride on the cart of Albert Buckingham behind the beautiful shire horse then going down Rooksmoor to the field in Frogmarsh where the rubbish in the cart was buried. My aunt and uncle later lived in the house by the field, but it was no longer used as the tip. Brenda Rimmer

Cheryl and I were on a rare trip out, Bristol Zoo around 1957

A Coop mobile shop similar to the one that would come to Kingscourt
(Photo: H G Creasey & Sons)

A similar green Morris 'J' type van (Photo: Wikipedia)

Holidays were always held during the 2-week factory shutdowns, that were the norm in those days. I barely remember the first one when I was three, we went with my mother's cousin, Glady's Dawson and her husband Charlie, to Scarborough, staying in a small caravan, and I mean small! The lights were gas with a mantle which dad had to change when they burnt out. It turned out that Glady's and Charlie weren't married, but they did eventually marry when I was a teenager!

The following year we piled six of us in dad's little soft top car and drove all the way to Looe in Cornwall. No motorways or town bypasses then and the trip took from very early morning until early evening, complete with the obligatory stops to get the Primus stove out and have a brew up on the side of the road.

Six up in a Morris 8, off to Looe in Cornwall. Mum, dad, Uncle Joe, Auntie Kitty, Cheryl and me. No seat belts, one windscreen wiper and a leaking roof - around 1957

Another year we went on holiday in the Morris 8 touring Wales, each night we would end up in a pub/inn with rooms. Mum, Cheryl and I would remain upstairs after tea and dad would be in the bar and was known to join in with the many Welsh male voice choirs if they were there. Towards the end of the holiday, we came home via Liverpool and through the relatively new Mersey Tunnel. Mum had been moaning at dad all morning and when we were in the tunnel he stopped the car, got out and stamped on his Trilby hat, then at the top of his voice he shouted, "I love my wife, I love her dearly". That kept mum quiet for the rest of the journey home – shock, or admiration?

The first Christmas I remember was when I was four, not sure why but on Christmas Eve I slept on the floor in my grandmother's bedroom, maybe dad didn't want to be woken up at about 3.00am with the noise of me opening presents, and what presents! My meagre package contained an orange, a small bar of Fry's Chocolate Cream and – a tin of Horlicks tablets. These were originally launched in the 1930's and were supplied to British and American troops during the Second World War as energy-boosting treats, but they rapidly became our 'sweets'. Then I found a small box at the foot of my bed with the words PIFCO written on it, what on earth was it? It was a torch, but a torch with a difference. Either side of the on/off switch was a slider – one green/one red. By sliding the bar up, you could also shine a green light or a red light, absolutely amazing for a 4-year-old. Gran wasn't that impressed though as dad had put the batteries in and I shone the torch around the room until the batteries were exhausted!

He got up early on Christmas morning and walked into Stroud to pick up a capon for Christmas dinner, I believe it was expensive in those days, and beef was cheaper then.

Pifco, my magic torch

I was born in Butterow and went to Rodborough secondary modern before it closed and pupils went to the new Archway School in Paganhill. I left school at 15 and started work at one of the many mills along the Brimscombe valley. They made wooden knitting needles and my job was to put the wooden heads onto them. When the Coronation was held in 1953 we had a TV, as we were also one of the first houses in Butterow to have electricity, it had a small 8" screen but the house was packed to watch it. Pam Hutchence

Lydiia Korotkova is a Swiss friend of mine who grew up in the Moscow suburbs, their buildings were centrally heated from a communal heating plant, as many still are in Russia, her childhood was much the same as ours, here are two of her stories:

I was 3 years old, and I left my grandmother's house, having tied my grandfather (a veteran of the Second World War) to the central heating radiator with the bows and belts from my grandmother's dressing gowns (grandfather was lucky that the radiators were not too hot). I suggested to my grandfather to play war, and "took him prisoner". I tied him up so that he would not prevent me from leaving the house to look for my grandmother, who had gone to the store. I dragged a stool from the kitchen to the hallway but still could not get a warm coat and hat from the hanger. Then I took my grandmother's big warm downy shawl from the chair, tied it around myself as best I could and left the house in the severe frost. I thought that my grandmother was in the nearest small store, next door to the house, but she was not there. Then I went to the big central store, which was far enough for a three-year-old child, and I had to cross the road on the way to the store (it's good that there were very few cars on the roads then). Luckily, there was a woman in that store who lived in our building, and she brought me home. My grandmother and grandfather were so happy to see me that they didn't even scold me. My grandmother blamed my grandfather, not me, I felt very ashamed and sorry for my grandfather, I hugged him and asked for forgiveness. I was really lucky, because I was lightly dressed in the severe frost, it gets dark very early in winter, I could get lost on the way and freeze to death, I could get hit by a car or meet bad people on my way. It was not in Moscow, but in the nearest Moscow region, in the city where I was born, the city of Dmitrov.

Even as a child, I really liked doing things on a dare. Once my friend Lena and I (we were 4 or 5 years old) argued whether you would get infected or not if you drink water from a clean puddle. Lena said that if the water in the puddle is transparent, it means it is clean, and you can drink it. She argued with me and drank water from the puddle. I did not want to lose the dare, but I also did not want to drink water from a puddle like a dog. I brought a medical measuring cup from home, poured water from a puddle into it and drank it, telling Lena that if the cup was medical, then all the microbes would die in the water in this cup. Soon we were both in the infectious diseases department of the hospital with dysentery (the medical cup did not help me disinfect the water!).

Daniela Kneubühler is another Swiss friend who grew up on her family farm in Rickenbach, Canton Lucerne. A very similar upbringing to many children here in the farming community.

This was my parents' home, from my grandparents. I had many aunts and uncles who always visited us. Sometimes they even spent a week with us and worked on the farm. Work was apparently everyone's hobby! They also went to church every Sunday; however, I didn't enjoy that, we already had to go to school for six days a week. Our way to school was 3 km and it was pretty hard in winter. Up the hill with the sled and down again on the other side. For lunch I was allowed to go to an aunt that lived next to the school. There was always a round table with ten people. My aunt still had two unmarried sister-in-law who also lived there and helped. It always smelled good for homemade Christmas cookies, and I think I like to bake because of it so much. However, I took always my own food with me. I was too shy to sit at the large table, and I couldn't eat everything either. I never loved meat, and I knew that they just filled their plates. I even go back and visit the farm because my mother and brother still live there.

Daniela's aunts and uncles on a sled outside the family farmhouse circa. 1920's, small children or massive dog!

FIVE!

Approaching my 5th birthday two events were significant – we were moving home, and I was about to start school. Dad worked as the Apprentice Supervisor at TH&J Daniels in Lightpill, an engineering company, now long gone. It transpired that the factory owned several properties in the area which were rented out to supervisory staff, etc. He was offered the upstairs flat at Greystone Lodge, which was bang opposite the Bath Road Post Office, now a Balti takeaway shop. Even though it was an upstairs flat it was bigger than my grandmother's house and I had my own room! The lounge and kitchen/diner were massive; the bath had a gas boiler above it for instant hot water and my sister had her own room in an annex. It was bliss and the Alderwick family in the flat below were very friendly too. Sadly lacking was the huge garden that my father had in Kingscourt, so he just kept on growing his fruit and veg there.

My father was Lithuanian and my mother Italian, we lived in the wooden houses as you left Slad Road heading up the valley, opposite the farm which is now the Peghouse Rise estate. Further below our house was a track leading down to an old factory by the stream, we learnt to ride our bicycles down the track but most times ended up in the brambles at the bottom. On one occasion I was walking back up the track while putting a broach in my mouth and promptly swallowed it. I rushed home to tell my father who said I must eat the potato pancake he had just made – nature would take its course which it did, thankfully there was no pin on the broach. Anna Karmilavicius

During this time Peter Cornish moved into the new post office which was at the very bottom of the Gastrells, a strange, whitewashed block building with a flat roof, and then by a quirk of fate his father took over as landlord of the Golden Cross, which is where you now find B&Q.

It was always arranged that I and Peter would attend Kingscourt primary school although both of us were in the catchment area for Rodborough primary school, strangely we stayed with Kingscourt. This threw up an operational issue – how to get there and how to get a midday meal. The Bristol Omnibus Company ran a single deck bus from Stroud to Kingscourt so that was simple, and my grandmother was going to provide lunch for me each day. Peter's mother arranged for my grandmother to feed him too, on the proviso that he brought something she could cook for him, easy really, it was a paper bag of some fruit and veg every day and she provided some meat.

First day at school. None of this pre-school stuff or mothers waving goodbye at the gate with tears in their eyes. About 8.00am and I stood at the bus stop right outside our house with my mother. She spoke to the conductor, not a band conductor but the man who took the money and issued the bus tickets, told him we had to go 'all the way', and that was that. Same happened in Walkley Hill where Peter's mother did similar. We got off at the top of Kitesnest Lane and dropped Peter's meagre rations at my grandmother's and proceeded to walk the remaining distance to school along with other children. We had no preconceived idea of what would happen next! Can you imagine parents today doing this?

Ushered into a room with low tables and benches, with no backs. We were told to sit down and were introduced to our teacher, Miss. Knight, who lived in North Woodchester. I think there were probably about a dozen of us and the names of most I remember to this day. Gary Hocking, Derrick Hill, Kenneth Miller, Roger Griffin and then the girls – Judith Kemp, Jennifer Didcot, Jennifer Short, Susan Stevens, Joy Edwards and Jeannette Phipps are names that I always remembered, which came in handy in 2019, but more about that later. We soon became great friends.

As the day progressed there were a few tears from some and then the girl next to me wet herself! I had never known this happen, but then why would I, the girl sat there in silence until Miss. Knight noticed, took her gently out of the room to clean her and the bench up, and the girl returned a few minutes later resplendent in a fresh pair of knickers – obviously a normal situation with new pupils.

Having been born in Nailsworth in February 1947, when deep snow was on the ground, I didn't go outside for the first three months of my life, there was no doubt that I would not be normal! I thought that water was cocoa and said so at every opportunity, including visits to Weston-super-Mare where salt water became cocoa to me. At the age of 5 my parents moved to Fern Cottage very near Daniels Engineering, where Dad worked and my sister was born in Dudbridge Maternity home. A few months later when it was time to go on my first day to school at Rodborough Primary, my Mum walked me up Walkley Hill to the Prince Albert and turned left down Rodborough Hill to the school. Sadly, I had forgotten that my parents were moving house that day to 'Stepeholm', Tabernacle Walk. So….. at 3.30pm I strode off back up Rodborough Hill, turn right and down Walkley Hill to Fern Cottage. I knocked on our apartment door with no reply? Mrs Cawthorne from the opposite apartment came out and explained to a weeping John that my parents had moved house. No phones, no cars and so Mrs Cawthorne walked me up to Tabernacle Walk where I was chastised for my lack of memory. Indeed, I was not normal! John Cook, Rodborough

I don't recall many things in those first few years but three come to mind. A regular visit by the 'nit nurse'. This was at a time when personal hygiene wasn't deemed that important, or so it seemed, but apparently head lice and nits were and still are very common in young children and their families.

They are not caused by dirty hair and are picked up by head-to-head contact. The nurse had a small fine-toothed comb and would comb through our hair looking for these little monsters, some found it a bit painful if they had knotted or matted hair, if any were found I don't remember what happened next, but I think the child was sent home with a letter for the parents.

A very early school photo. L-R at the front is Judith Kemp, Judith Hocking, Joy Edwards, me squinting, Eira Savage and Susan Stevens. I can't recall those in the back row but the girl behind me may have been Gillian Ireland

Then the vaccination programme. Starting with Polio – a sugar cube on a spoon soaked in the vaccine. Later we had Diphtheria vaccinations, it is an acute and highly contagious bacterial disease causing inflammation of the mucous membranes, formation of a false membrane in the throat which hinders breathing and swallowing, and potentially fatal heart and nerve damage by a bacterial toxin in the blood. It is now rare in developed countries. This vaccine was combined with Tetanus & Pertussis (whooping cough).

All these inoculations didn't stop me contracting Chickenpox though. It is a highly contagious viral disease, and a rash typically begins on the face, scalp, and trunk, then spreads to other parts of the body. The rash can appear in stages, with new spots forming while others are developing into blisters or scabs. A high temperature is common, often preceding the rash. The entire illness usually lasts about 4 to 7 days, and the scabs typically drop off within 1 to 2 weeks. Nowadays it is treated with paracetamol-based medicines, when I caught it, my mother bathed the blisters and scabs with Calamine lotion which was supposed to stop the itching – but it didn't, I just ended up with pink blobs all over my face and body from the Calamine. If you burst the blisters or scab there was a real danger of the infection spreading further so this was discouraged, but how do you stop a 6-year-old from scratching an itch? Solution, knitted woollen gloves tied on at the wrist, scratch to my heart's content but the blisters wouldn't burst.

Other weird treatments too at this point. For a very bad cough – Wintergreen warmed in front of an open fire and rubbed into my chest. Heavy cold and blocked sinuses – Vick's vapour rub, and I still swear to it to this day. The final one was a septic cut or graze – a hot poultice, lint cloth soaked in boiling water was rapidly applied to the wound and wrapped in a bandage, by a miracle when the bandage was removed the poultice had drawn out all the infection!

Finally, the dreaded school dentist! Some wizened old man who had no doubt been struck off by the General Medical Council would poke and prod at your teeth before giving you, if you were unlucky, a 'letter' with two answer slips. This was taken home and your parents decided if you would go with the black, 'I am happy for this dental treatment to be undertaken by the school dentist' or the red, 'I do not wish my child to undertake this treatment by the school dentist'. The first time my parents sent back the black slip, and I hated having a filling. From then on whenever I got the letter, I always took it back having 'forged' a signature on the red slip. My own stupid fault really as in my teens I had terrible teeth!

Myself and Jonathan were always round the street and on the Common. Like most of the kids we used to dig up star stones from the end of Kingscourt Lane leading to the Common. This one particular day, we found our Dad's magnifying glass and took it up to the Common. Fortunately (or unfortunately), it was a very hot day and we were experimenting with the magnifying glass and tried to make a little campfire. It worked perfectly, except for the fact that the little campfire got out of hand and a very, very large area of the Common caught alight. Jonathan remarked to me years later that my face was one of horror and shock. Fortunately we managed to keep it under control.

Once, when in class at Kingscourt School, I was told, as was the whole class, that the next day there was going to be a spelling test. On the way home I was conjuring up a plan to miss next day's school. We had a barn in the garden leading down to the school, which was full of hay bales. After tea I went into the barn and using the hay bales made a hidden den, put in some crayons and paper, which would keep me occupied whilst I hid there next day to miss the spelling test. I had an Aunt who lived in a caravan directly opposite the Nag's Head at Bowl Hill which was all fields then, not built on. It was my Aunt who found me hiding. I can't remember what happened, as I must have been reported missing from school. I can still remember a man called Mr. Click who was a truant officer but on this occasion, I don't remember Mr Click reporting me. Neil Critchley

We used to have 'PE' or Physical Education on the tarmac playground. In the entrance hall to the classrooms were a range of pegs, each with our name underneath and a net bag to put our 'daps' or pumps in. We would strip down to our vest and pants, girls vest and knickers, put on our daps and take a coconut mat out. Not sure what we did on them, but it didn't kill us, it was good to get out in the fresh air. On several occasions we would even walk up Bowl Hill and play rounders above Little London.

It wasn't just all about school though, new friends appeared. Malcolm Robinson and John Poole from Middle Spillman's, and John Bond whose parents kept the little shop just below the Golden Cross pub, now also demolished, and living just outside Stroud threw up some more opportunities too.

Saturday mornings were usually a trip to the Gaumont cinema to see, for 6d (2.5p), a cartoon, some basic adverts and then usually a cowboy film – all in black and white. Once again, only about 6 or 7 years old but we went on our own, one stern word of warning though, 'don't go near the canal'. What did I do on returning from the cinema one Saturday but to go down to the canal at Wallbridge Lock, just below the Bell Hotel, to have a look – and slipped on the grass towpath and fell in. It wasn't deep where I went in, so it only came up to my waist, but I was wet and very muddy. A smack or two when I got home and those words were uttered once more, and a smack from my father when he came in from work too.

Cynthia, Doreen and I used to play outside in the road, sitting on the wall outside Boot Cottage where we lived and many times ended up falling off the wall into the stinging nettles. We used dock leaves to treat them! We also learned to ride our bikes round the lane. We used to have a tin bath on the wall outside which came in for Sunday bath night and Mum boiled pans of water for the bath. We all three took it in turn using the same water! We didn't have an indoor toilet but we had potties under the bed at night and a toilet up the garden in daytime! Jennifer Little (Didcot)

Another trip into Stroud would be to go train spotting, armed with the latest Ian Allen train spotting book I would studiously cross off the locomotives I saw and on one occasion my father gave me a task to complete.

He was a toolmaker/engineer by training and in his spare time he was building a scale working model of one of the Hall class locomotives, then he reached a sticking point, he wanted to know how many rivets there were around the firebox and so I was dispatched to the station, paid my 3d for a platform ticket (yes pay to just go on the platform) and waited. A couple of Castle class locos came through and the infamous Chalford 'Rattler' push me/pull me small train that did a regular run from Chalford to Gloucester and back stopping at the many 'halts' between the two, a bit like bus stops. Then a Hall came into view, and I raced down the platform towards where the engine stopped, almost at the very end on the Merrywalks viaduct. The driver could see me peering around the front of the engine as best I could, but I couldn't see them all, so he climbed down and asked me what I was doing. After explaining he climbed up onto the front buffers and counted al the rivets for me – good man!

We would go out in the morning and come home for lunch, go out after lunch and come home at teatime, I don't remember being asked where I'd been. Could have been anywhere in the village, I'm certainly not going to admit to anything now. One time after arriving home late, despite being told not to, I lied to my father about being stopped from coming home by some bigger boys. He suggested we went straight to see Constable 'Chalkie' White at the village Police House and report the matter. I chose to lie more wisely after that. Tony Sinfield

On my 6th birthday a party was held for me in the front garden and much cake, sweet treats and 'pop' was consumed. On waking the following morning I had a terrible stomach-ache and eventually my father called out the doctor, honest, they did house visits then if you called them, and it was a Sunday morning too.

He poked and prodded my tummy, which by now was unbearably painful, and suggested I may have appendicitis, so an ambulance was called, and I was taken to Stroud hospital – not casualty this time but straight up to the children's ward where I was promptly examined by a surgeon and rushed to theatre. Nowadays an appendectomy results in usually only a 2 day stay in hospital, in 1959 it was a whole 8 days. One issue there has plagued me all my life since. We never ate fish at home for some reason and after a few days we were given boiled white fish, mashed potato and parsley sauce – one mouthful and I refused to eat any more, and don't eat fish to this day!

I was at Woodfield Primary School, Dursley. My love was P.E., my hate was maths. On one particular day I had a terrible maths lesson, rubbing out incessant errors, eventually rubbing a hole through the page of my notebook. The teach was furious, she shouted at me that I wouldn't go to my next lesson, which was PE, I would stay behind and do additional maths. I had never been shouted at and was very upset by this incident, also at missing PE, so during lunch break I put on my coat, walked out of the school without telling anyone, and went home. I knew it was wrong and I hid in my room under my bedclothes waiting for my parents to return from work. A few minutes after I got in, the phone began to ring. We had a Trimphone with a high pitched ring, but there was no way I was going to answer it. After a while I heard the front door open and mother saying "Mandy, are you here?". Reluctantly I wandered downstairs with a tear stained face and described the incident. Mum took me back to school where she told the teacher in no uncertain terms never to shout at me again and that rubbing a hole in a page was hardly a punishable offence! Mandy Williams

At around 10pm on the night of Friday, June 30th, 1961, described at the time as a "beautiful mid-summer night" – moonlight from the cloudless sky was later lost in a "brilliant orange glow" from the flames. The Ritz cinema which stood where the Merrywalks Shopping Centre now is was ablaze. Tucked up in bed with my teddy I was unaware of any of this until my mother burst into my bedroom and woke me up and hurriedly dressed me, we could see the glow in the sky looking from the back of the house over Lower Spillman's and my mother, father, sister and I went up to the brow of the road and looked down into Stroud and could see the fire blazing out of control. A report in the 'Stroud News & Journal' at the time stated, "It appears the fire started in the roof of the cinema – the SNJ suggests the culprit was an overheated electric motor operating an extractor fan. In fact, before fire services were eventually alerted by two inspectors at the nearby bus station who had spotted smoke, people attending the last showing at the Ritz smelt burning towards the end of the programme. It was not until 10.19pm – ten minutes after Mr Waters locked up the Ritz with just the cinema's kitten, Tiger, left inside – that firefighters made their way to the scene. And what they found: "great spurts of flame spouting in unimaginable fury," according to the SNJ.

Residents – mostly teenagers – soon gathered to watch the spectacle. Included in the crowd was Sid Griffith, who had just landed the job of chief projectionist at the cinema. "I thought: Oh no, don't say I've been burnt out of a job after such a short time," he later recollected. Despite the drama, the fire was successfully contained, with no lives lost or serious injuries.

And yes, that even includes Tiger, who was found hiding in the ruins of the cinema's toilets the next day."

Two days later an excited Malcolm Robinson came calling for me, he had a secret! He had been cycling up in Rodborough Fields and found a complete roll of cinema tickets, the sort that came out of a metal plate in the foyer desk when a foot pedal was operated, the rising heat and wind effect had lifted it up into the air then deposited in the field. He had taken it into the wood store of the builder's yard in Middle Spillman's, opposite his house. He showed it to John Polle and me and announced his cunning plan; we would use them to get into the Ritz to watch films once the damage had been repaired – they demolished it.

The Ritz burns! (Photo: Stroud News & Journal)

Remains of The Ritz (Photo: Stroud News & Journal)

We used the wood store as our den, crouching on the ground to get under the wooden gate, then smoking those green hollow weeds that grew everywhere, that I don't know the name of. We could have burnt the store down!

Sadly, about 12 or so years later some boys, all from the same Woodchester family, entered a barn in Rodborough Fields and did something similar, but they started a fire, and one was unable to escape, tragically leading to his death. As an assistant cub scout leader at Rodborough, I attended the funeral in Woodchester, so utterly heartbreaking as he was in my cub pack.

Mealtimes were an adventure as we weren't rich by any standard, my mother worked for local solicitors Winterbotham, Ball & Gadsden in Rowcroft but we didn't necessarily have a great income. It was not unusual for me to have ketchup sandwiches and dip butter in the sugar bowl as a snack, however, food preservation was high on the list, and we bought a fridge. It had one of those mini freezer compartments at the top and she bought a packet of frozen peas, they came loose in a cardboard box, anyone remember them? Another swing back to hard times was the bowl of 'dripping'. It came out, some was scooped in a frying pan to cook whatever, and any residue was poured back in the bowl. Gross by today's standards but my father would layer lashings of it on bread and eat it – no wonder he had heart issues.

We would though have a good fried breakfast on a Sunday, it was my father's job to cook it and at the time we also had a budgerigar in the kitchen, and it would fly around the room, until it landed on the fried bread in the pan. I thought we may have had more protein that Sunday but with a burnt foot it flew back to its cage, none the worse for wear.

My 3rd friend in Switzerland is originally from the Philippines, and we met when I was in Switzerland celebrating my 70th birthday. She grew up in Malabon which is about 30km from Manila, the capital.

I can tell you something about what my parents did when my siblings (10 of us) and I were little. When a beggar came to us, he not only got a few cups of rice, he was also able to eat with us. During storms/monsoons our neighbours were able to take refuge with us. My parents were so kind and showed so much empathy and compassion. Hermie Schmid

Yet another trip to casualty came about when the end of my finger became swollen and painful so in came my uncle Arthur, who was also in St. John Ambulance, to give a diagnosis. I believe it was known as a Whitlow, which is also known as herpetic whitlow, a viral infection of the finger, typically caused by the herpes simplex virus. Treatment today, obviously, is antibiotics. No such luck for me, off to casualty and one injection in the tip of my finger – ouch! Then two either side and my fingernail was cut off. Bandaged up and sent home with regular dressings back at casualty.

I lived in Newmarket Road, Nailsworth for the first 21 years of my life till I got married. We had a ' Wireless ' of which dad was in charge. Washing machine! That was done over a scrubbing board in the sink then put through the mangle. The tumble dryer was the washing line, and if still damp, the washing was put on a clothes horse, a fireguard put round the fire, and it was left to dry off when we went to bed. We did have an iron of sorts and an ironing board which more often than not collapsed on to our feet. My gran had no electricity she ironed with a very heavy ' Flat Iron ' that was heated on a ' plate' by the side of the fire. Of course, there was no fridge everything was stored in a dark cupboard along the back wall, in the kitchen. We had a small fishpond and in the Summer string was tied round the top of the milk bottles, and they dangled in the water to keep cool. As our mum said, " where there's a will there's always a way". Kerry Thomas (nee Payne)

By now at the early age of seven my middle name had been changed from 'Albert Frank', as decided by my very imaginative parents using the first name of their own fathers', to 'Mischief'. If I could get into it I did, those words again repeated many times, and the smacks continued. I know corporal punishment is frowned upon now in a nanny state, but my mother would very occasionally hit me with a bamboo cane, can you ever imagine, friends would get hit with a leather belt!

John Poole lived in a block of Victorian terrace houses in Lower Spillman's, one day when his parents were out, we climbed up through the loft hatch into the roof space, there were no firebreak partitions between each house so we could get into other houses through their loft hatch too – so we did. We cautiously dropped down through one into another house, had a good look around, and then went back. To get back up though we had to stand on top of the sideboard, which was strategically placed underneath the hatch, I wonder what the owners thought when later they looked and saw footprints on top of it!

Enough was enough – one afternoon when my mother came home from work, she told me we were going out, this never happened as we would be thinking about having our tea. We walked down through Strachan's Mill at Lodgemore and across the railway line at Beards Lane and up to the technical college. What fate was awaiting me? Turned out it was a sort of trade exhibition for young people to get a glimpse of what may be waiting for them when they left school. I wondered at the Army stand with guns, etc. and then the RAF one had a German Shepherd guard dog, and more on that later too. I spent an enjoyable two or three hours there with her and promised from them on to be good, well for a few weeks anyway.

School was good and I did enjoy the small class numbers at Kingscourt. Rounders up on the common as we had only a small tarmac playground. In summer we would pick rose hips from the hedgerows, and they were sold to a syrup manufacturer, I don't know who got the money. There were other charity type events even then. We would get a little book of 'Sunny Smiles' which had a photo of a child smiling. It was to raise money for children with cleft palates. People could donate and get the photo in return – weird! Finally, 'Pestalozzi' fundraising. The Pestalozzi Children's Village was established in Trogen, Switzerland, in 1946, after the Second World War, to accommodate and educate children from both sides of the war. The concept soon spread to other countries, and in the UK the Pestalozzi International Village was a charitable organization and residential educational centre in East Sussex, that operated from 1957 until 2019. It provided scholarships and a nurturing environment for disadvantaged children from around the world. We would pay a donation of 1 shilling (about £1 now) and in return we received a little Ladybird badge!

In today' educational system we cater for children with 'special needs' but no such opportunities for many children out in the sticks. Two school friends of mine were in a way disadvantaged. Jonathan Critchley contracted Polio early in his childhood and had such weak leg muscles that he had special boots with leg irons connected again at the knee. It looked terrifying and poor Jonathan would sway from side to side when he walked. In later life he became a paramedic in Stroud, no longer had leg irons but his swaying gait never went away. The other one was Trevor Marks who was very if not nearly totally deaf. He wore a little pouch around his neck with an amplifier and two wires up to his ears, it also looked very antiquated and basic. Once a week he was taken from, school to what was, I presume, some sort of therapy session but usually returned an hour or so later. I met up with both of them again in 2019.

One thing that really upset me was being almost forced to learn to write right-handed, as I was predominantly left-handed. Coming home from school that day I was in tears and when my father came home from work, I told him why. No sooner did I tell him that he marched me out of the house and back up to school where Mrs.Cox was packing up for the day. In no uncertain terms he told her that if I wanted to write left-handed then I could, job done!

The Pestalozzi Ladybird pin badge

The good old days, out all day with friends, home for tea, bath and bed. Well bath once a week! 😄 *A sixpence each for pocket money, that bought us a packet of sweets and a comic from the corner shop . Dad bringing his wages home in a brown envelope on a Friday and putting it into different pots for the bills and grocery money. Camping at Charmouth, Dorset - 2 adults, 3 kids, a dog, a tent and all the equipment in a Mini traveller !! Fantastic holidays, life was simpler and no mental health problems like today. Mandy Brown*

The overloaded Mini traveller of Mandy Brown's father at Charmouth (Photo: Mandy Brown)

At Christmas it was the Nativity Play, I wanted to be Joseph, but I ended up as Herod, which quite upset me as I knew he was a 'baddy'. Dressed in my pyjama trousers, slippers, dressing gown, a tea towel on my head held in place by an elastic belt I don't think I matched the real image of Herod from the Bible.

This late 1960s photograph shows young pupils of the former Kingscourt School, near Stroud, presenting a nativity play for parents and friends.

Look how pleased these children are! A few years after I left but still the dressing gowns and tea towel head covering (photo: Remembering Rodborough)

I was at Minchinhampton Primary school circa 1956/57, I cut a chunk of my hair off and another classmate cut a hole in his jumper so were not allowed to have craft scissors in class, I was about six! I hate potatoes and refused to eat them, so was put into first sitting at primary school, then was made to sit all through second sitting while others played, then Mr. Boseley would come over, hold me while Mrs. Walker force fed me! My pal Sally was so scared it would happen to her she hated peas so would hide them in her knickers! - This was maybe fall out from strict rationing and lack of food in the war, we certainly were told we must eat all. In end of 60's during college holiday I delivered meat for Taylors. Orders were on grease proof paper on trays in the back of the van, no fancy cling film, shrink wrap, etc. Oxtail, in case you do not know, has lots of bones running down, so when ordered it's a slice, imagine all bones with meat around and slice tied with string. I arrived in Amberley, grabbed it, and it fell apart, so there I was trying to fix it all like a jigsaw puzzle! Sue Workman (Bartlett)

Winter also brought another issue, the outside toilets. They were at the far end of the playground, the boy's urinal was open to the sky, the toilet seat was basically a wooden hole over a pit, I presume we had a cess pit underneath but I also recall there was a big black pipe exiting the playground wall running down towards the Kings Head. In winter the water in there froze, a nightmare. Next to it was the coke pile for the 'Tortoise' stoves that were the only heat in the classrooms, or classroom. I say classroom as this Victorian school had a very high ceiling and one room with a shuttered partition to turn it into 2 classrooms. Badly fitting metal window frames and drafty holes – and just the one stove, we were tough in those days.

I was promoted to coke monitor, a grand title for a boy who had to go out into the playground in all winds and weather to fill the coke scuttle!

I grew up in Bagpath, near Kingscote. We lived in a cottage with no electricity, no running water or sanitation. We walked down a hill to collect drinking water which was dipped from a well and then carried back up the hill in a white enamel pail with a blue rim. We were the lucky ones as my grandparents at the farmhouse a mile away had a bathroom with (slightly) hot water heated by a coke fired Rayburn which was stoked up on Saturdays for the weekly bath. Tim Sage

The post war baby boom is reflected in this picture of Kingscote baby show, 1948

Christmas was always a great time, as I went to two organised parties. Daniels Engineering held one each year in their conference room with lashings of food, games and party presents and the Tabernacle held one in the room with the stage (where the Rodborough Tabernacle Players featured their many plays). One attraction there was a magician, and I love magic to this day!

After leaving Hoffman's dad got a job with the Britannic and progressed through the company, moving around and retired at 62. Dad made ends meet by doing children's parties as a children's entertainer in magic. He had a trick catching pennies and with a rabbit.....and entertained around the county. He became a member of the inner magic circle. Dads Father got him interested, I think. Grandad was more into card tricks, but I remember a man called Serle who with Dad did a Chinese act with a chopping machine, but that was for adults! Linda Bell

Mrs. Cox was our new head teacher, and she would stoke up the stove until the top almost glowed dull red, until one day she did this and after about an hour smoke started to escape from the wooden wall covering behind the stove. Fire alarm, what fire alarm! The other teacher ran down to the phone box at the bottom of Bowl Hill and called the operator (there was no dial as the Stroud exchange was a manual one, so you didn't dial 999, for an emergency call there was a big white button on the back board to press if you needed the emergency services) – press it she did. In the meantime, we were ushered out into the playground after collecting our hat and coat from the annex, and the fire engine arrived. It was the same as the affectionately known 'Green Goddess' but obviously red. The wooden panel behind the stove was still only smouldering but to us it was the pinnacle of an exciting day!

Tortoise Stove (Photo: Wikimedia Common)

The type of fire engine that attended that fateful, but exciting day (Photo: Flickr/Mick)

When not at school we would keep busy at play. Up on the common we would play 'Cowboys and Indians' (now probably called cowboys and indigenous American people), cops and robbers and the ever best – English and Germans at war – all with our invisible guns. We even tried Doctors and Nurses, but I was too immature to understand what that was about – no not really. Just a bottle of water with us and when we got hungry, we would eat berries or apples until it was time to venture back home for a real tea. Many a time we would have cut legs and arms from running in and out of bushes and grazes where we had fallen over – the remedy was simple, into the bath with a good portion of Dettol added, germs neutralized and smelling good!

The Hungarian Uprising of 1956 was a spontaneous nationwide revolt against the Hungarian People's Republic and its Soviet-imposed policies. Triggered by widespread discontent with communist rule, the uprising began with student demonstrations and quickly escalated into armed conflict with Soviet forces. Despite initial successes, the uprising was brutally suppressed by the Soviet military, resulting in thousands of casualties and a renewed period of Soviet control. Many refugees ended up at Rodborough Fort and quite a few settled here afterwards. I remember in my early years at school several Hungarian children came into the upper class, so we never really mixed, but I always remember them coming in through the school gate in bare feet, so poor I thought. In the late 90's I was talking to a builder who happened to say he was one of those children, I mentioned the fact they were so poor they had no shoes, he laughed and said, 'we took off our shoes to walk across the common as the grass was always wet, we put them back on after arriving at school' – who would have thought! My sister, Cheryl, being older than me mixed with the children and can recite the Hungarian numbers even today.

Church still featured in our life. Every Sunday morning after breakfast I would get sent packing to Rodborough Tabernacle, sit completely bored in the main chapel for about 20 minutes then get paraded off with all the other children to 'Sunday School'. This was even worse but what could I do, I was under strict parental instructions so that was it, every Sunday. To brighten things up there was a girl there from Dudbridge called Marilyn, and I liked her. So, one Sunday walking back home to Bath Road (yes still walking on our own) I took Marilyn home to introduce her to my parents as my girlfriend – I think the relationship lasted a week or two.

The 1946 School Milk Act had required the issue of a third of a pint of milk to all school children under eighteen and this was a nice thought if not always a pleasant experience. In the summer it stood outside in the sun and it was warm and thick because this was full cream milk, not the semi-skimmed coloured water that we have today, and in the winter it had a tendency to freeze and pop through the foil cap in an arctic lump that had to be sucked away before you reached the semi-liquid slime underneath.

1/3rd pint bottles of free milk and waxed straws (Photo: Historic UK)

No one knew about lactose intolerance in those days, and it was compulsory for everyone and there were always teachers on hand to make sure that everyone finished their drink of milk whether it made them ill or not.

EIGHT!

Just when you think everything is going nicely more change. My father had a 'falling out' with one of the senior managers at TH&J Daniels and basically told him to stuff it, and then he resigned. No roof over our heads, my parents took out their first mortgage and we moved into Chandos Road. Number 55, a relatively new build, 3-bedroom semi-detached property.

Again, I had my own room, a small pokey box room above the stairs, my sister had a bigger room at the back. We had a lounge/diner and a kitchen, that was basically it.

I was born in 1952 at Tetbury Hospital, and I lived there until 1979. I had a wonderful childhood with my mates from infant school to secondary. Out all-day during school holidays. One of our favourite places being Escort Park, the large house was still up then. There is an island in the middle of a lake. We built a raft, 6 of us with 5-gallon drums and wood tied together with string, all materials we borrowed from local farm sheds on way down, not one of us could swim. But as kids in those days we did not see danger. We used to cook potatoes on open fires. Potatoes were picked from local allotments. No one bothered us. Les Lye

A new experience came about soon after we moved. It was a cold and wet October evening and after tea my mother pulled a green sweater over my vest and placed a green and yellow striped cap on my head. The sweater was on the large side, my mother said, "you will grow into it", and very itchy against my bare skin. However, my raincoat went on and my sister walked me a mile or so from Chandos Road, up Tabernacle Pitch to that same Rover Hut. Twenty-four years after my father and mother attended the opening, I was about to start my own adventures in Boy Scouts as a Wolf Cub.

The hut was barely visible at the bottom of steep steps leading through undergrowth to the door. Going inside I was struck by the smell of damp wood and a log fire. About 10 or so other cubs were there and at the far end of the room I saw a small totem pole with a stuffed wolf toy at the top. Branches from the totem pole had paper discs hanging from them. My name was added to a disc and hung on the pole – I was in!

Throughout the coming years I became a 'seconder' then a 'sixer'. A seconder had a metal star which was pinned to one side of the scout badge on his cap, a sixer had another star placed opposite side. Apparently, this signified the maturing of the Wolf Cub, as we were known, with first one eye opening and then both eyes – why seconder and sixer I never found out, except a sixer led his "pack" of wolf Cubs and a seconder was his deputy!

My time with the Cubs was great and we played brilliant games. One that would be forbidden now was British Bulldogs. The object of the game is for one player to attempt to intercept other players who are obliged to run from one designated area to another. British Bulldog is characterised by its physicality (i.e. the captor inevitably must use force to stop a player from crossing) and is often regarded as violent, leading it to be inevitably banned. Most commonly one or two players – though this number may be higher in large spaces – are selected to be the 'bulldogs'. The bulldogs stand in the middle of room, all remaining players stand at one end of the area (home). The aim of the game was to run from one end of the room to the other, without being caught by the bulldog(s). When the players are caught, they become bulldogs themselves. The last player is the winner and starts the next game as bulldog. The odd graze or bruise was a small price to pay for having so much fun.

We took part every year in 'Bob a Job Week' – more like child slave labour! Cubs and Scouts would knock on doors and ask if anyone wanted a job done, for a 'Bob' or 1 shilling (5p). This ranged from weeding, washing a car, dusting, cleaning windows and at Mrs. Miller's in Kingscourt Lane it was always polishing the horse brasses and brass candlesticks. Much elbow grease required and ended it with foul smelling black fingers from the 'Brasso' – and just for a 'Bob'!

At this time, I met Frederick (Eric) Daniels, the great grandson of Thomas Daniels the founder of the engineering company of T H & J Daniels. Eric was Group Scout Leader, having started the scout troop as a Sea Scout unit. Eric was, to be frank, a little eccentric, but 100% a good scout and leader. His dress code left a little to be desired but that added to the eccentricity. One night at flag break we noticed that Eric had the fly undone on his shorts, quite a surprising thing to see as an 8-year-old, but never fear, another Cub manoeuvred himself in front of Eric and attempted to do up the zip – what a disaster, Eric was mortified and accused the boy of undoing it – fun times indeed.

I still met up with my friends from the Bath Road, normally in the Rodborough Recreation Garden next to the church and Endowed School building. We would ride our bikes in and out of the bushes, grapple with the girls (in the bushes!), make a lot of noise and climb trees. We rarely saw any adults there. In the centre of the garden was a massive pine tree, but I couldn't climb it as the branches were too high up to start. Armed with dad's hammer and a bunch of nails I placed then strategically into the trunk to give me a hand and foot hold up to the lower branches, and away up I then climbed, right to the top. Easily 30/40 feet up and if I fell, I would probably have broken my neck!

We settled in Tabernacle Walk at Stepeholm, next door to 'Stalcot' where my Grampy Cook and Auntie Lottie lived, I began a lovely life of playing cops and robbers on the Common, building shelters in Grampy Cook's wood and generally mucking about. We played bows & arrows and shot them at each other until Gordon caught one in the head and his Dad banned us. So, it was back to the Common where we had seen men with caps and badges setting fire to the Common in a very official way. Mike said that looks like fun and so we pinched a box of matches and went up to the back of Tabernacle Walk and started to set fires all the way along to the pitch which ran down to Rodborough Tabernacle! We got a bit scared when a police van turned up and we all hid behind a bit of upstanding common. Sadly, we were found and plonked into the police van and taken to the police station to await our judgement aged 9. Our parents eventually picked us up and berated us, as they should, but with a smirk! We never did it again! *John Cook, Rodborough*

John, on the far left, sledging with his mates down from Rodborough fort in 1957

At this time the council started to build houses at Fishers Way and Little Fishers, Kingscourt. For an eight-year-old and his friends we had a new playground. After dinner we would descend on the building site, climb scaffolding, explore rooms shooting at the 'Germans', hiding in foundations and generally having a good time. However, we broke asbestos sheets, fell in water filled trenches hit our heads on scaffolding poles and then I trod on a nail sticking up through a plank of wood, a very big and long nail. Limping home it was time for my father once again to take me to casualty at Stroud hospital. A tetanus injection and a dressing and sent home and told in no uncertain terms never to go on the building site again, but of course I did.

A few evenings later and a knock on the door and when it was opened we saw our neigbourhood policeman, in those days you were very frightened to see one – they were the law! Apparently local children had been playing on the building site and doing damage, nothing to do with me I said, and a very strange look from my father.

I grew up in Cirencester and lived in a street made up of Cotswold stone cottages with a post office, a grocers shop, a greengrocers and a butchers. They were all independently owned with the exception of the Post Office. We used to buy huge bags of broken biscuits for a penny. No expense spared! One of the shops didn't have a till or a cash register, you just put the money through a slit in the counter. We never cheated!!

Foraging was not a word we used but foraging we certainly did on a daily basis while wandering the lanes. We ate elderberries, lime tree leaves, and hawthorn berries which we called bread and cheese. The only way we children kept in touch with each other outside of school was by knocking on their front door so if you had friends in another part of town you walked to their house to see if they could "come out to play". Jane Quilliam

When I was about 9 years old my parents rented some ground and a smallholding not far from Stinchcombe. One afternoon we went up to Dunkirk, just below Badminton, to collect a load of straw that that been baled that day. My job – I had to drive the tractor and trailer from stack to stack while dad and mum loaded all the bales up onto it. As the layers of bales got higher, mum and I would go on the top of the stack while dad pitch-forked the bales up to us. Once the trailer was loaded, I had to catch the ropes that dad threw over the top, then make sure he caught them the other side, and he would tie them all down. I had to shimmy down the ropes back to the ground and off we went, load by load back to the smallholding. It took us till almost midnight to finish the whole field – farming was no easier in those days. Mandy Williams

My ninth birthday approached, and my father said it was time I got myself a job, was I leaving school so young? No, it was normal for children to have a Saturday job or similar, e.g. a paper round, working in a shop, helping get the bottles from the cellar for Peter's father at the Golden Cross – I was going to be a milkman! Bert Browning lived next to Rodborough Tabernacle, his wife was the cleaner there and he was the caretaker and local milkman. Working for Stroud Creamery, which was at the very end of Lansdown, where Little Mill Court now stands, its round' started in Bath Road, covering the whole estate of Kingscourt Lane, Hillclose estate, Kingscourt and the Street.

He would start around 5.00am and finish around 2.00pm, I would meet up with him at the start of Chandos Road about 7.00pm. In those days we delivered three types of milk – normal, extra creamy (Jersey milk) and sterilized, along with eggs and orange juice. On a Saturday it was payment day, so I had to collect money and ensure I gave the correct change, and my reward after 7 hours work – a half a pint of milk to drink and 10 shillings (roughly £10 by today's standard).

This I did for 5 years in some of the worst winter weather, but I never complained – or got a pay rise!

One customer was Mrs. Miller again in Kingscourt Lane, she kept German Shepherd dogs, but I never had issues with them, until I was leaving one day and one of them lurched at me and sank its teeth into my 'bum'. No real apology (until my father went up there later and told them a few home truths) but Mr. Browning took me straight home and my father then took me, yet again, to the casualty department at Stroud Hospital – I was becoming a regular. This time it was dressed but not until I had another Tetanus jab and a very painful Penicillin jab in my bum, think that was more painful than the dog bite though.

My brother Paul and I arrived in Rodborough on Christmas Eve 1959. We'd come from a London suburban estate with small gardens, close neighbours and the flat landscape of Essex. Rodborough was quite a shock – first of all to our house movers, who took one look at the steep path up to our house and almost turned round to drive back to London. Luckily my mother persuaded them to unload the furniture, otherwise we would have spent Christmas on the bare boards of our new house.

Our first school was Rodborough Infants – and a huge change from our bright, modern purpose-built school. I'll never forget the shock of discovering that the toilets were in the open air across the yard! Kingscourt became our next school, where my mum was a teacher, and for the first few years we had to walk across the common and down Bowl Hill or cut through the field at the end of Tabernacle Walk.

Our life as children had a much gentler pace than today, but there was enough to do to keep us busy. We made much of our own fun, climbing trees, playing war games and making up treasure hunts in our rather wild garden. TV reception was poor on our side of the hill, so our main indoor entertainment was reading and board games, looking back at the family photos it was a great childhood – a safe, relatively car-free environment, with plenty of fresh air and exercise, and time to use our imaginations to avoid boredom. Geraldine Wooley

My big brother Tony and I did shopping for an American couple in our street, Gloucester Street, Cirencester.

This photo shows Tony and I at the window of the lovely American lady who rewarded us with a trip to the Circus. I also remember collecting cigarette butts from the street for another American lady who stripped them down to make cigarettes to smoke. The American airmen living in our street stationed at Fairford used to throw away long, long, cigarette butts. Perfect for our cigarette lady!! Jane Quilliam

Jane Quilliam (Townsend) as she was in 1966, a teenager still

The wedding of my cousin Sheila Wilkins to Bert Moffatt at Down Hatherley Church, Cheltenham. L-R Granny (Phyllis) Wilkins, Grampy (Albert) Wilkins, dad, me, Cheryl and mum

The winter of 1963 will long be remembered by myself and no doubt many others who were alive at that time. The snow started falling on Boxing Day 1962, with a belt of rain in northern Scotland turning to snow and moving south. This marked the start of one of the coldest and snowiest periods in the UK for over 200 years, known as the Big Freeze, which lasted into March 1963. On the morning of 27th we didn't know what had hit us! It was still hammering down and up to the windows, drifting heavily in the high wind, and it just kept falling, as did the temperature too.

We may have been living in a relatively modern house, but we only had single glazed windows, an open fire with a back boiler for hot water. We kept the coal for the fire in a 'coal bunker' outside the back door. I don't remember coal being delivered but my father kept that fire going day and night for weeks. We put ex-army brown blankets on the bed along with our normal winter quilt and flannelette sheets and I even wore a sweater in bed and a woolly hat! In the morning, I would get up and go to the window, there would be ice on the inside and the curtain stuck to it in places.

Worse was to come. Arriving at school after the Christmas break we found Mrs. Cox in her Triumph Herald stuck on Kitesnest Lane, although she had got that far from where she lived in Birdlip, so we all dived in behind the car and pushed her to the top and on to school where the other teacher already there told her that all the pipes were frozen and the toilets not functioning. By now the school had a telephone and after a few calls she made an announcement. The school was going to close – hurray! We were going to carry on at Rodborough School – boohoo. The canteen at Rodborough was hastily reorganised with extra tables, chairs, etc. and we began a daily route march to school, about a mile each way but in snow that was up to the top of our wellingtons. When we got home though the fun would begin.

We had our fair share of snow in the 1960's, and living amongst the hills and commons in Rodborough and Kingscourt we were able to enjoy proper sledging at a steep angle and at speed from The Fort all the way down. Shrieks of laughter when we fell off. Boys putting snowballs down the girls' necks. Building snowmen - all great fun.

Most Saturday mornings my mother and I caught the number 56 double decker bus from Stroud to Gloucester for my piano lesson. Mum would disappear to the shops! In those days not only was there a bus driver but also a bus conductor in his uniform, complete with cap, and who chatted cheerfully to the passengers. He had a machine that issued everyone with a ticket when he turned the dial and then a handle – fascinating to watch.

One Saturday in the winter we motored slowly out of the town, past Whitbread's Brewery and on up the hill towards Edge, looking out of the windows and enjoying the ride. Our heads were not stuck in our mobile phones, texting. As the bus chugged slowly round the bends snow began to fall, then the bus got slower and slower, eventually grinding to a halt: Engine failure! We were well and truly stuck. The snow kept falling slowly. The children got excited, the adults a little anxious. Eventually we were all laughing and chattering thanks to the cheery bus conductor who led us all in singing carols and Christmas songs. It was a memorable journey thanks to our public-spirited bus conductor. *Jennifer Hardy (Short)*

The period of a full moon in a clear sky with white snow made visibility at night almost as good as daytime. After tea we would all rush out with our sledges and trapse up to the stile at the top of Gastrells field. It was a great run down to the bottom, then back up and do it all again. With no idea of time, we would go home usually when we were cold and soaking wet. Woollen gloves, a duffle coat and long socks and shorts weren't ideal, but when I got home my mother would put all the wet clothes on the fire guard and they would steam away all night!

When the moon had gone, we sledged down the road at Court Way by streetlight, until a man came out and told us off for making too much noise, so we did it down Fishers Way instead.

I was born in Aldershot in 1937 and the winter of 1947 was one of the coldest of the Century. The snow was deep, and we built barricades 6 feet high for snowball fights. The only heating in our council house was an open fire grate in the living room. As kids we had to take an old pram down to the gasworks in Ash Road to get coke (which was cheaper than coal) to mix with the coal for the fire. The coal was stored at the back of the house opposite the toilet which had no light in, until my dad wired up a torch bulb and battery to give us a glimmer of light. Woe betide us if we forgot to switch it off as the battery would soon run down. Ken Ellison

Pram loads of coke leaving Gaythorne gasworks (Photo: Mirrorpix)

When we moved into the house my father started to build a garage, by the winter it had 3 walls but no door or roof, but his Morris Oxford was parked inside and now completely covered up to the roof in snow. As the thaw began, he firstly charged the battery and then removed the spark plugs and put them in the oven. All nicely warm he put them back in the car, turned the key, and it started first time – amazing.

Hand-me-down clothes. Although I was a girl, I still inherited many clothes from my older brother. Jumpers, anoraks, etc. were pretty much considered unisex and I do not think I had a new pair of wellingtons boots until I was about 12, when my feet stopped growing at size 4 and my brother's boots were too big even with extra thick socks! Homemade knitted clothes were also prevalent during this time. My grandmother spent hours knitting jumpers, scarves, mittens, and hats for all the family. There were even matching outfits. I am sure not many children today would be happy wearing this. It is not clear in the photo but even the trousers were knitted. We played with Spirograph, Etch A Sketch, Play-Doh, Fuzzy Felts, puppets (I had Dougal, Brian, and Florence from the Magic Roundabout) slinky and clackers. The most inappropriate sweet available then must have been "sweet cigarettes." Jane Cox, Amberley

Jane resplendent in her fully knitted outfit, around 1966

Jane's elder brother Nicholas was the one who provided the 'hand-me-downs', this is one of his reminisces.

Growing up in Amberley was amazing but getting around was a nightmare with the number of places that you wanted to go within walking distance less than the number of fingers on one hand. You either had to cadge a lift from parents or cycle. I could cycle all day on the flat, but that was a problem. From Amberley, you can't cycle more than two miles north before the geography interferes with you travel plans, yes you can freewheel down into the valleys, but it's a long push back up the hill!

So, I used to explore southeast, it's flat all the way to Cirencester and beyond. I got to know all the lanes and villages – Sapperton, Coates, Tarlton. But the valleys kept calling me, Slad, Painswick, Golden Valley. And the places beyond, Cranham, Cowley, Arlingham – all inaccessible if you didn't have an engine.

On my 15th birthday I resolved to get an engine, you could buy a brand-new Yamaha moped for £212 and I had £12 in savings, leaving me with 12 months to raise £200, so I got a job at Minchinhampton Motors working the petrol pumps at the weekend for fifty pence an hour.

For many, MOTs were aspirational rather than actual paper documents and one client had repaired his petrol tank with fiberglass and connected the petrol cap to the tank with a length of radiator hose and two jubilee clips. He asked for five pounds worth of petrol, a lot in those days when fifteen pounds was a typical take home weekly pay packet. I cheerfully rammed in the nozzle and let the petrol gush but stopped suddenly when I realised my feet were getting wet. I'd dislodged the bodged hose and squirted five pounds of petrol into the boot of his car!

I had two choices, tell him and risk a bloody nose and thick lip or keep quiet. It wasn't a difficult decision. I took his fiver and cheerfully waved as he drove up Windmill Road leaving a trail of wet petrol in his wake.

Twelve months later I got my moped, and the world was my oyster. Even today, I love the smell of a two stroke in the morning. The smell, you know that unique petrol and oil smell? The road to freedom is best travelled on two wheels! *Nicholas Cox, ex-Amberley and Parliamentary candidate in the 2024 election for Hertford and Stortford*

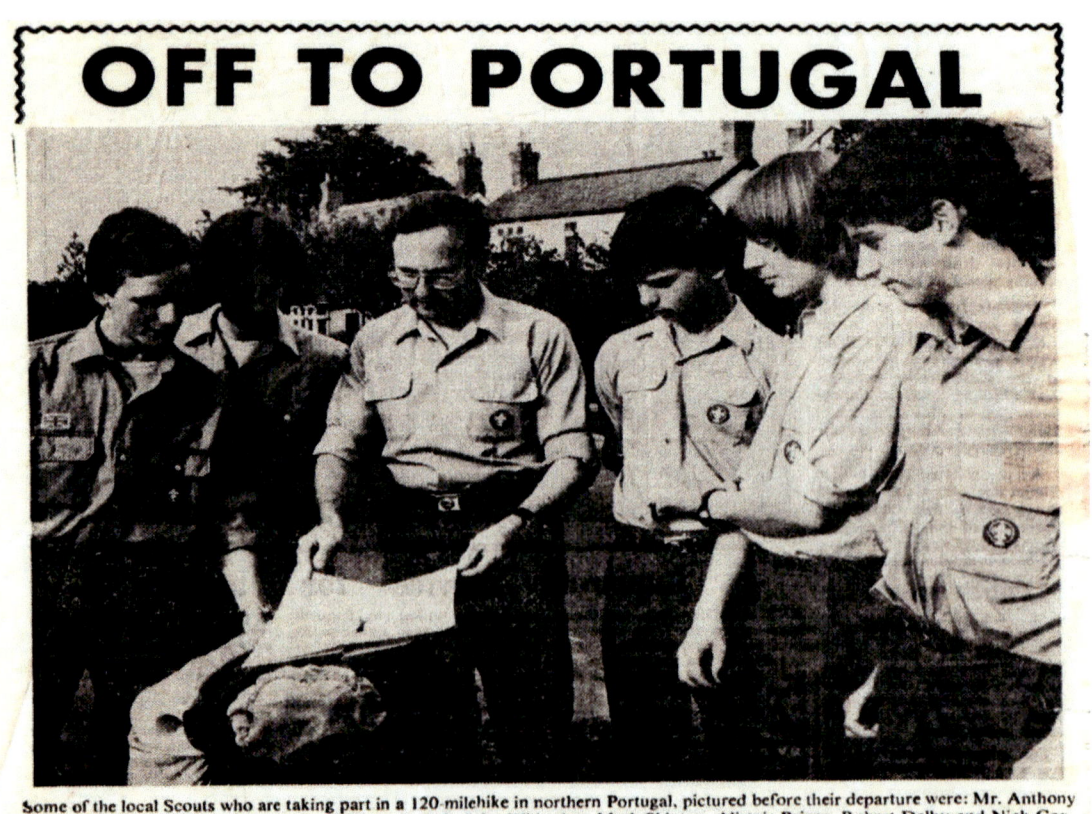

In 1978 Nicholas 'Nick' Cox was a local participant in the Explorer Belt Expedition to Portugal, here with other local Scouts. (Photo credit: unknown, possibly Stroud News & Journal)

PE time around about 1962, and daps and coconut mats. No vests, pants and knickers by then, real PE gear!

1964 and I was about to leave primary school, but first we had to sit the 11 plus examination. We had three choices for further education based on our results. The brand new secondary modern at Archway School in Paganhill, the Boy's Technical School in Beard's Lane or the Marling Grammar School in Downfield Road. I ended up earmarked for the boy's Technical School, along with my best friend Peter.

Many days in Cirencester were spent playing in the river Churn at the bottom of our family garden, but the most fun we had was sitting in the gushing lock gates splashing each other laughing all day !! We didn't check our watches every few minutes to see what the time was. We played until we were hungry. There was excitement in the air on our street on more than one occasion, the first one was a rumour of a bubble gum machine being installed in our street down by the shop. The second one was a slide was going to be erected in the play ground about half a mile up the road. The chidren from estates at the other end of the town flocked up after school to see this wondrous new slide. Our side of the town became very popular. Jane Quilliam

I lived in Tuffley and would meet up with my other friends and sneak off to the new store being opened behind the New Inn in Gloucester. We were about 8 or 9 years old. There we found a set of new supermarket trolleys so what to do with them? A multi-storey car park had also been built for Eastgate Market and there was an entrance/exit ramp down into Station Road. We jumped in the trolleys and raced off down the ramp, then realized they couldn't be steered. We hit the walls, barriers, each other and some turned over before we got to the bottom. Great fun but someone no doubt had to collect the trolleys! Stephen Molden

Upper school, pre-11 plus exam – Mrs Cox surveying our work, I'm just off centre left sitting next to Susan Stevens, also in the picture Gary Hocking, Geraldine Woolley and Jennifer Didcot (Photo: Remembering Rodborough)

Next was a big surprise, we were all scared (well at least I was) a little by Mrs.Cox but she invited all the school leavers to a party at her house, which was at Birdlip. At just 11 years old we caught a bus to Stroud, then a Cheltenham bus which went via Cranham and Birdlip. Not a parent with us, the brave gang ventured out into the wilds. She met us opposite the Air Balloon pub, now gone, and we walked across the fields of Crickley Hill and deep into the wood, then we came out into a field and a beautiful Cotswold stone cottage. We met her husband who continued to feed us and top up plentiful glasses of pop and played games all afternoon. The last time we saw her but a grand send off for us 11-year-olds as we ventured forth into a bigger world!

Travelling on our own on public transport held no fear. My friends and I often rode the Nailsworth – Stroud route for a few old pennies, on our own or in a group. Catching the bus at the long since demolished Golden Cross pub at the bottom of Walkley Hill.

In those days we had freedom. We were free to explore, to run errands to the local shop. We were happy and imaginative, too, playing on the common all day; hide and seek amongst the trees and bushes ; running up and down the dillies; collecting as many things as we could put in a match box. Not an adult in sight, no 'health and safety.' We were allowed to pick huge bunches of cowslips, especially when it was the Sunday School Anniversary at Rodborough Tabernacle. A group of us loved decorating the woven baskets with lilac, cowslips, and cow parsley; all ready for us to carry them at collection time during the service. We dressed in our 'Sunday best' and it was the only time we went in the chapel gallery as there were so many people attending. Jennifer Hardy (Short)

Do you remember the old Kingscourt school? When the school couldn't cope with the increasing number of children, around 1969/1970, my parents offered to have a school terrapin hut placed in our garden. We were in the next house up from the school, (Laburnum). Once built the teacher had to line us up and we walked up the hill through our garden gate to get to the terrapin. One day my Mum was confronted with a huge spider in the upstairs bathroom. She bravely tried to pick it up in a mug, then panicked screamed and threw it out of the open window, landing on poor Mrs. Cox who was leading the children through. Mum said Mrs. Cox screamed and ran for her life. Poor Mrs. Cox! Lyn Thompson.

ELEVEN!

First day at Stroud Boy's Technical School. Long grey socks, grey shorts, grey flannel shirt, school tie and grey blazer. It must have cost the earth. Peter and I went in through the gates together, no parents, I had gone on the bus from Lightpill to Beard's Lane, Peter I think had walked. We were introduced to our form teacher and spent the day writing out our class programme and handing over 2 shillings to the dinner lady. This indeed was going to be interesting as I had never eaten a regular school meal, only a few when we decamped to Rodborough in 1963. Lunch time and into the canteen, eight to a table with an older boy at the head in charge. We would have to go to the serving hatch and collect the tray of food for our table and likewise for our pudding (or dessert as you now call it). Some of it was OK, some was absolutely dire. The gravy would stand up on its own, the meat wasn't the best cuts and the vegetables steamed to within an inch of destruction. Pudding was blancmange, jelly, apple pie (which was OK) and lumpy custard. I soon learnt that if I wanted to get a substantial lunch then I would have to eat all the things that the others shied away from, how much cabbage can an 11-year-old eat, or salad. Friday, oh my God, fish! "Pleas sir, I don't eat fish" so I was given two thin slices of the mildest cheese in existence, and this went on every Friday.

School life was now much stricter and I soon grew to like some teachers and hate others. For English we had the Rev. Cook. He was a submariner during WW2 and I presume he became a man of the cloth afterwards. I didn't like him and then I disliked him even further. He gave us homework, and we had to take it back the following day. He chose pupils at random to read out what they had written, I had written nothing, and he picked on me. I tried to bluff my way out but an 11 year old against a WW2 veteran, I had no chance. The punishment came next, "tonight you will write a 1,000 word essay on having the 'correct tools for the job'" I could have cried.

I spent all evening up until bedtime but managed to do it. I went up to his desk and handed it over the following day. He didn't even look at it, he ripped it up and put it straight in the bin. Lesson 1 learnt!

We used to race each other on our push bikes from the Quarry to Stringers Close – the finish line being our garage at 9 Stringers Close. This required the negotiation of left-hand turns from Walkley Hill into Courtway and into our drive in Stringers Close. The former often had a participant ending up in the front garden of 2 Court Way, the latter cycling through Dad's prize roses on failing to make the turn. To spice things up we often took on the turn into Kingscourt Lane rather than Court Way (an even tighter turn) or a quick shimmy around Southgate Crescent and back out to Courtway.

When one of us got a speedometer fitted the challenge was to take the Court Way corner at 40 mph. How we ever survived not coming off a bike, let alone colliding with a vehicle shows how little traffic there was on the roads – this would have been early 70's. We also made go-carts and raced down Court Way turning right into Stringers Drive with a spotter at the junction to ensure no cars coming from either direction. Steve Pegler-Major.

It was now goodbye to Cubs and hello Scouts. A tradition then, was to be pulled from Cubs into Scouts across a broom handle, which represented a river. After saying goodbye to the Cub pack, the Scout leader or a Scout would grab your hand and pull you over the broom – I sadly cannot remember the significance of this ritual but remember it happening on many occasions.

Boy Scouts were a totally different 'kettle of fish'.

In my new uniform of khaki short sleeve shirt, khaki shorts, and long brown socks I proceeded from Rodborough up Tabernacle Pitch once more, but this time to the Scout Hut, if you could call it that. It was the converted coach house beneath the Little Chapel opposite the Tabernacle. However, on arrival I was met by about 6 or so Scouts running towards me from the hut. Apparently, the District Commissioner had arrived to disband the troop, to this day I don't know why, and one of the Scouts had put a 'banger' up his car exhaust pipe. Bang, and I joined the other runners, my introduction to Scouts lasted less than a minute.

Eric Daniels was distraught that the troop had been shut down and wanted to keep it going. So, several months later Nicholas Sutton, Derrick Hill, Chris Marks and I met at Stringers Court, Rodborough – the home of Eric and his housekeeper. I had never been in this imposing house before, situated in large grounds complete with a pond, bamboo jungle, stables, and long drive. I had seen it before from Stringers Farm next door as we would spend summers there as children helping farmer James and Geoff Weaver bring in the straw bales, and scrogging apples from his orchard! This was different though, as once inside, and to my surprise it felt like stepping back in time – even further than the house I grew up in. Dimly lit, dark colours, old furniture, and the sort of smell you always associate with old things.

We were given pale blue neckerchiefs that night and Rodborough Scouts lived to fight another day. For several months we would meet in his kitchen and sit while he told us stories from the Boer War, the history of Scouting started by Baden Powell on Brownsea Island and skills which we never knew existed – knots!

Finally, we went back to the Scout hut under the Little Chapel. My first night there I thought this is a total tip. Double coach doors in the middle, 2 windows either side and that was pretty much it. Lockers and cupboards at one end of the room, large open fireplace at the other – just like the Rover Hut it smelt damp and dreary. We could though light a fire and plenty of wood surrounded the building, roaring fire and all the dreariness forgotten. Our Scouting education continued, and we shortened "Skip" (Skipper from Sea Scouts) to Kip, he didn't like it. We would hang from the ceiling on ropes and listen to his stories with growing admiration. Eccentric, definitely – incapable, never. He became affectionately known as Uncle Eric by us all.

Then one evening we were introduced to a new member of the troop, John Marks who was to become our new Scout Master under the watchful eyes of Uncle Eric.

John was a revelation. I can say that in the following 4 years he shaped my character and helped me become the person I am today, not necessarily compliant but we had a Scouting introduction which in part had driven me to write about the whole 26-year experience, my 3rd book, "Dehydrated Chicken Supreme and other great Scouting Adventures".

June 1965 District Camp at Whiteshill
L to R: Judith Kemp (1st Rodborough), Helen Alder, Jennifer Short (1st Rodb),
Alessandra Matthews, Mrs N. Harvey (Quarter Master enjoying tasting the main course),
Mrs. D. Keane (District Commissioner), Diane Alder, Jennifer Didcott (1st Rodb)

When I went up to Scouts, Judith Kemp, Jennifer Short & Jennifer Didcot moved up into Guides.

A few of my Kingscourt School ex-pupils were in Rodborough Guides, if I am correct, it is L-R Linda Bell, Cynthia Didcot, Susan Lusty (Rodborough School), Jennifer Short and Pauline Stewart (Photo: Remembering Rodborough)

I shudder in horror now at the things we did! We went hedge diving after dark diving over people's hedges. 'Knock down ginger' was played by tying cotton to people's door knocker, trailing it out to the gate, hiding round the hedge and pulling it to knock the door. Then we ran away quickly before we were caught. The roughest game of all was called 'jump a nagger' (nagger is slang for horse = a nag) where 5 or 6 boys would line up rugby scrum style with one boy standing at the head against a tree. The other team of boys would take it in turn to run and leap as far up the line of boys as possible with the others following. The object was to collapse the line of boys in the scrum. Ken Ellison

Dad had left Daniels and gone to work for Sperry Gyroscope at Bonds Mill, Stonehouse, in the drawing office. Now a 'blue collar' worker. His income had increased significantly too. My mother had transferred to the Stonehouse branch of WB&G and got an improved salary, they were on the gravy train at last, and so was I!

Allen's was still a paper shop as sweets were still on ration. The only sweet we had was Spanish Root a sort of twig that tasted of liquorice. Bookmakers were illegal and Mr. Allen ran an illegal betting shop to which I had to take 2 shillings (10p) wrapped in paper and say, "spot" sent me! It was my dad's way of making a bet! Ken Ellison

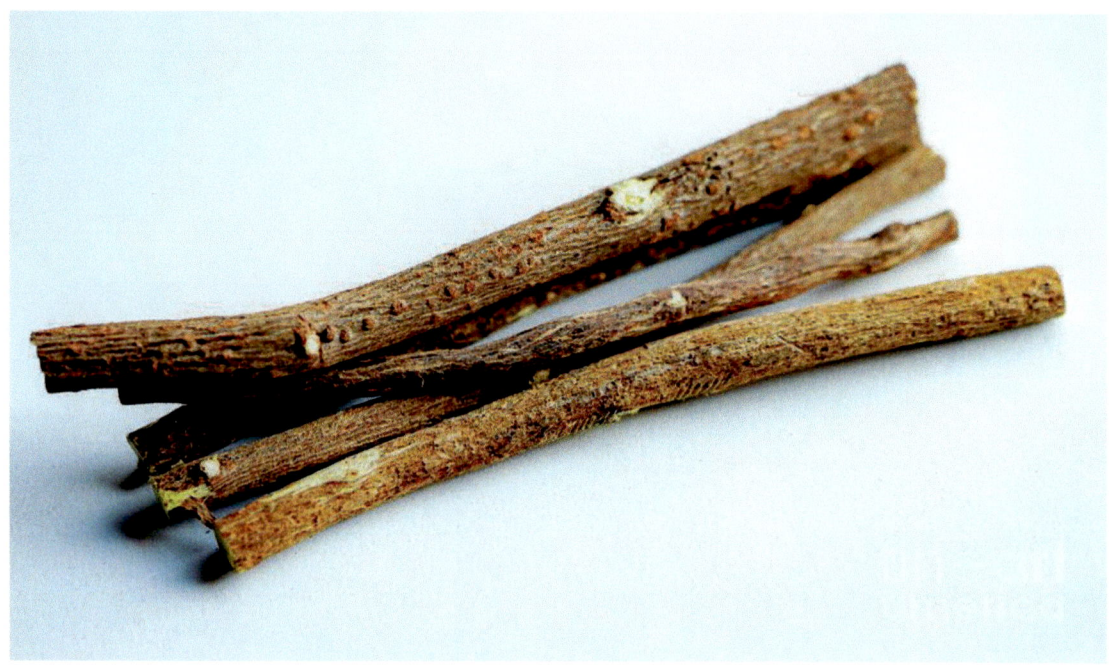

Spanish Root – yummy!

Getting up at 5.30am was not a good feeling for a 12-year-old, except I had hardly slept all night as I was about to embark on the greatest adventure of my life, a coach holiday with Beavis Travel. My father and mother packed our small suitcases into the car and along with Cheryl we headed off to Bussage for a 6.30am start. The coach looked new and amazing, and we had seats right at the front. My sister and I behind Madge Beavis who was sitting in the "courier" seat and mum and dad behind Brian Beavis who was driving us – and off we went!

Southampton, a ferry port, I had never seen one of those before or seen a ferry so large. I had been on the King Harry ferry across the River Fal in Cornwall but there was no comparison, this one was gigantic, this was a Thoresen ferry, Viking 2.

The Thoresen group was set up in 1963 and was led by Norwegian Otto Thoresen, he had worked for a number of years as manager of Fred. Olsen's Mediterranean operation, garnering experience in the freight and ferry business. During that time he had become increasingly frustrated at the amount of inactive time ships under his tenure spent between voyages and the time-consuming, arcane freight handling methods employed at each port. He was convinced that he could do better, utilising a roll-on roll-off freight containerisation system. He also felt that this could operate in tandem with a more streamlined method of transporting passengers and cars. Viking 1 and Viking 2 were virtually identical and both entered service on 19th/20th July 1964, so was only a year old when we ventured onboard. In April 2011 she sank after the tug towing her to the breakers collided with a drilling rig. The Thoresen group went on to become Townsend Thoresen.

Thoresen Viking 2, small by today's cross channel ferry standards (Photo: ShipSpotting.com)

I think it took us about 6 hours or more to get to Le Havre in France but what a time we had. Mum got seasick before we even left Southampton and gave her handbag to my dad and said for us to go and get something to eat. Being a Norwegian ship the dining was a little unusual to say the least, Smorgasbord was dominant. It is very practical food that can be made in advance and caters to different flavours. It is Nordic style tapas and consists mostly of cold cuts, such as smoked salmon and scrambled eggs, skagentoast and cured meat. Avoiding this we dined well on steak and chips, but mother didn't seem to want to join us. We left Le Havre and after a couple of hours we reached our first overnight stop in Abbeville. Brian unloaded all the suitcases, porters took them to all the different rooms and Madge shepherded us all into the dining room where we ate our first ever foreign meal, I can't remember what it was but I know mum didn't like the soup as it was clear and watery! I had to share a room with my sister who was about 18 years old then, the hotel had strung a curtain across the room between our 2 beds for privacy. I remember the windows wouldn't open but it was a hot night. Lesson 1, abroad the windows open inwards as the shutters are pulled across outside.

The toilet and bathroom were across the landing, and one had a word on it that for some strange reason I thought sounded rude, the sign read DOUCHE (SHOWER, as I learnt years later when I was taking French at school). The other strange thing was the soap in the bathroom – it was banana like in shape with a hole through its length to enable it to be bolted to a wall fitting, who would want to steal the soap I wondered?

Continental breakfast – what can I add to the description, these days very few will not have had one of these, even in a UK hotel, but to me with no cornflakes I felt betrayed. However, after a warm croissant, butter, jam and the biggest cup of coffee I had ever seen, more like a soup bowl, I was ready for adventure day two.

Mum struggled in asking for a cup of tea, even worse when it came without milk. Dad searched high and low for the bacon and eggs!

We set off for our second overnight stop in Nancy, after a couple of hours stopping in Reims to see the Cathedral. After a lunch magically conjured up in a roadside restaurant by Madge, unless she had booked us in advance perhaps, we set off once more only to grind to a halt in a layby after strange noises appeared underneath the coach. Brian soon shaking his head as he appeared back into the coach to announce that the spare wheel carrier had parted company from us, those French roads were worse than ours are in the UK now. Dad to the rescue, you can never go wrong if you have an engineer on board and some nifty work with some wire and all was good. The overnight in Nancy was pretty much like the first in Abbeville, I was getting into the holiday way of life, I even helped Brian remove all the suitcase and put them back on the following morning.

Day three, off to our holiday destination in the Swiss Bernese Oberland, Interlaken. Going via the Ballon d'Alsace (didn't see why this was anything to do with a balloon but apparently in later life I realised that it was the name of a mountain pass). Finally arriving at our hotel in Interlaken called the Weisses Kreuz, which apparently translates to White Cross, the Swiss flag emblem, again something I didn't appreciate until later life. This time to my delight the hotel had a lift, and I had my own room – bliss, the room was good too. Dad told me off for keep going up and down in the lift!

353 NAA, the coach I went to Switzerland in, here at our hotel stop in Nancy

A lunchtime halt somewhere in France, Cheryl and my mother on the right waiting to reboard the coach

The whole Switzerland experience was so amazing that it has stayed with me ever since, my first book was even all about Switzerland and more than 70 visits I have taken throughout 57 years. While in Interlaken we took part in many trips – Harder Kulm, Trummelbach Falls, Lake Brienz by paddle steamer, Schynige Platte, folklore evenings and best of all, to the 'Top of Europe'.

Top of Europe, this was the Jungfrau mountain - the reason this mountain in the range including the Eiger and Mönch, is so famous world-wide is its railway - Jungfraujoch is the highest accessible point in Europe - up to a staggering 11,332ft (3,454m) height - thanks to its centennial railway, which was inaugurated in 1912. One morning our hotel gave us each a small cardboard box, wondering what it was I opened it. A packed lunch – fruit juice, bread, cheese, ham, cake, orange, apple, chocolate and a paper napkin. This was living! The journey to the top of the mountain took about 3 hours by train, exiting at the highest railway station in Europe, buried deep underneath the Jungfrau.

My father was a pipe smoker, much to his dismay his pipe wouldn't stay lit on the Jungfrau due to reduced oxygen at the high altitude. That was a good laugh! I believe the trip cost about £40, today it is more like £300 from Grindelwald/Wengen – and grossly overcrowded.

On our return trip we headed to Porrentruy, stopping off on the way to visit Bern the capital. While there we visited the bears in the bear pit, which didn't impress me that much as they looked pretty miserable and scruffy. Then on for our overnight stop in a beautiful hunting lodge style hotel deep in a forest on the outskirts of the town. Before dinner, as I now knew it had to be referred as, the owner offered everyone a sample of local wine in his wine cellar, but we were all standing in the entrance lobby? Then, as if by magic, he rolled back the heavy carpet to reveal not just a trapdoor but a wide staircase leading underneath us, these weren't Tesco style wine racks, here were 1,000's of bottles and barrels. During the second World War the owner's parents, who had the family hotel then, needed to ensure that their extensive wine collection did not fall into German hands, so they excavated under the hotel to make a new and larger cellar. Depositing the "cheaper and newer" wines in their existing cellar the good stuff was hidden away under the carpet – so simple but it worked.

The impressive north face of the Eiger, taken in 2013 from Kleine Scheidegg on my 60th birthday European Road Trip!

On then to Rouen for our last night in France, a long day this one as we stopped in Fontainebleau to visit the opulent Fontainebleau Palace. Built by French royalty, with parts dating back to the 1100's. Even though I was only 11 years old this was jaw dropping, I had never seen anything as rich and ornate before.

Finally, the last day back to Le Havre, Southampton and home, mum ate on the ferry this time as she said dad spent too much buying us lunch on the way out! Duty free shopping on board was limited as there were strict rules about how much sterling could be taken abroad, so even a bottle of whisky or pack of cigarettes was going to be difficult to purchase – so my dad didn't bother.

On my return from Switzerland a new shock awaited me, my school had amalgamated with Marling School and so it was new uniform (again) and new teachers, as well as trekking between the two schools for different lessons. We had to play rugby in winter and cricket in summer and I hated sport, even worse we did cross country – across Cainscross Road, through Lodgemore Mill and up Rodborough Hill to the Fort and return, I wasn't going up that steep hill so darted into Middle Spillman's and then tagged back in when everyone else came back down the hill!

The curriculum was different to that of the Technical School, concentrating more on the academic side of things and I hated it, especially French, which I still haven't grasped to this day, even though we holiday in France most years now. 'Ticker' Mildmay was the French teacher, they always have nicknames, no idea why 'Ticker'. In our class were three Wilkins – Alan, Brian and myself. Ticker referred to us by first names so it was

Alan, Brian but not Melvyn, my forename initials were MAF so he called me Maf, a nickname I was to maintain until 1988!

The very last Stroud Boys Technical School photo in 1965. I am front row 2nd left, Peter Cornish is 2nd row 1st left. (Photo: Russ Cooper – Stroud Boys Tech archives)

We would have been about 11 years old and quite a good gang of us. Behind the Kings Head was a storage area where the empty barrels and bottles were placed awaiting collection by the draymen. We would sneak around the back, collect as many cider and beer bottles as we could carry then pop in the front door and claim the deposit back on them! We would then buy 'pop 'and sweets and any money left over we put in a tin that was placed behind a brick in the wall of a demolished house in Rooksmoor Pitch. Climbing on the wall to retrieve it one day I fell and broke my arm, the boys made a splint out of two branches from a bush and tied it with vine before taking me home - which was only about 50 yards further up the pitch. My father didn't own a car, so we walked back down the pitch to catch a bus to Stroud hospital. Peter Hocking

Sunday at the Tabernacle still featured and now somehow, I had been enrolled into the choir, but it did have an upside Carol Singing. I and Nigel Carter would trudge all the way from Rodborough, up across the common and onto the Private Road and The Hithe, all in darkness. These houses were the home of the rich, even by today's standards. Architects, consultants, bankers, high powered business owners, etc. We would be up there for about 3 hours or more and made an absolute killing, those we missed the first night we attacked the following one. Best of all was when we got invited into a massive house where a Christmas party for the adults was being held. We sung our hearts out with about 4 carols and they all dipped in to their pockets and we got £'s, on top of that cake and snacks and a warm drink – result!

…but it isn't just us village kids who had fun and did silly and sometimes even stupid things. John Faulkner was born in Birmingham in 1965, and it appears city kids were no different either, here a few of his misdemeanours:

I remember using a WW2 bomb crater on the side of the hill in a park for riding my bike down and jumping high out of the lowest side on the hill, and hitting my head on a tree branch whilst 8ft off the ground, that

hurt, I couldn't see properly as everything was a blur, so had to walk my damaged bike home in the dark for an hour, told my parents nothing about it, and went straight to bed.

I also remember exploring a large water pipe with friends, maybe 3ft in diameter, in which we crouched along for at least 1/4 mile in the dark before deciding maybe it wasn't a good idea, seemed fun at the time.

Finally there was the time I cycled with friends half way across Birmingham to Cannon Hill Park, on the way to which was a really tall metal children's slide, had to be at least 20ft high, with a metal ladder to climb to the top, lots of fun, except the gravel rash at the bottom, it was set in concrete for 'safety' !!! Nobody died.
John Faulkner

N.B. I remember very similar experiences on the slide at Stratford Park, Melvyn Wilkins

FOURTEEN!

After 5 years it was time to change jobs, dad knew the manager of Halfords bike shop in Gloucester Street, Stroud and got me a Saturday job. This was more like it! No rain and cold, a warm(ish) old shop with a cellar in which a wizened old man made up the bikes that had arrived packaged, I don't think he ever saw the light of day. Predominantly sales were cycle related but the chain, excuse the pun, was moving towards the automotive section as well. I had learnt a lot from my father watching him working on his cars and therefore this introduction fitted well with me. I understood what someone wanted when they asked for feeler gauges or contact points and could easily reference the part from the several catalogues that were there, nowadays in Halfords you have to find it yourself!

A month or so after starting we moved into a newer and larger store in King Street, this was better laid out and we had a girl there who worked on the till, Lucy was about 8 years older than me, but I was smitten!

As kids we never washed our hands much, so I contracted Shigella Dysentery which nearly killed me. I was aged about 12 and my temperature rose to 113F (45C) overnight, I was completely away with the fairies - the doctor came to our home in his Rolls Royce (he was an amazing Hungarian who'd managed to get out during the war, but his surgery had walls covered with prints of the most diabolical vintage surgical instruments) to give me an injection to knock me out for 24 hours, I took months to recover. Perhaps I picked it up from a coke bottle, or something the cook might have touched (the staff had a house at the bottom of the garden, of our home, it had a rudimentary chain flush loo and shower / taps) but everyone would come and go there. Nick Dunn, Blantyre, Malawi

1967 and we moved again, literally by wheelbarrow. When the housing estate was built the contractors had their site buildings on the plot of land on the corner of Heather Close and Chandos Road, once all the houses were built down came the site buildings and the last house replaced them, dad decided to buy it when it was finished and we moved the 3 doors up from 55 to 61, by carrying almost all our belongings ourselves.

This new house was a nightmare for dad, he loved his gardening, but it appeared that almost everything the builders didn't want was buried in the front or back of the house. He had to dig hardcore out at the front so that he could lay a lawn and the back garden, well, we found a sink, taps, metal pipework, bricks and half a cement mixer! One thing it did have though was central heating, oil fired with a tank out the back, luxury at last. A few years later it was double glazed throughout as well. My bedroom was upstairs at the back whereas my sister had a much larger one downstairs at the front. It was probably supposed to be the dining room, but our lounge was so big we used it as a lounge/diner.

One Sunday evening my father was taking my grandmother back home after supper and I said I would go along for the ride. I sat in the back of his Austin A35 and tried to open the little quarter light window, it was jammed so I gave it a bit of a shove with my hand. A pain shot up my wrist and I could feel a wound and blood, but it was dark, so I told dad to go without me, and I went back indoors. In the light I was horrified. I had a deep 4" gash across my wrist and blood was pumping out, I had severed an artery. Mum passed out so Cheryl grabbed a towel and wrapped it tightly around my wrist and we waited for my father to return. He put a torniquet around my upper arm and telling me to keep my arm raised we headed to Stroud casualty once more.

Stroud had just introduced a one-way system down Rowcroft meaning we had to go all the way around Merrywalks and the rest of the town to get to hospital. Dad decided against it and drove the wrong way up Rowcroft!

At the hospital it was decided that I should be transferred to Gloucester by ambulance and they were about to start setting up a drip for blood when a GP doctor stuck his head around the door to see what was happening, apparently no doctors were working in casualty on a Sunday evening but he had been visiting a patient. It was decided that instead he would stitch my wound and save me going to Gloucester. Nine stitches later and I was now in deep shock, and home we went. I had the next day off school with weeks of my arm in a sling and it was my left arm – I attempted to write once more with my right hand, disaster.

I have vivid memories of summer evenings walking up to the lonely tree, as we lived at Hillside Terrace just off Rooksmoor Pitch. We all went on evening walks Mum, Dad, Chris and I up Bowl Hill through Little London, past the dew pond and the whole common was lit up with glow worms. It was like a mythical landscape. Dad would have us hunting for star stones (these star-shaped objects, resembling snowflakes, are actually a type of fossil, they are just a few millimetres in diameter and are fragments of the mineralized stems of sea-creatures known as crinoids. Resembling plants, crinoids are actually animals related to sea-urchins and starfish, and still occur in some modern seas), as it was a sort of half-light of the evening. He assured us that this was the place he had found some when he was our age. Needless to say, we never did. As the Autumn evenings approached, we went on the same family time walks only this time it wasn't glowworms that greeted us but a magical sky of red and blue soldier moths filling the air with every footstep. I've taken my children back at similar times only to find glowing fields and a magical sky, but they are no more. Stephen Marks

There were two items of clothing that my mother gave me for school, and I hated them. String vests - the string vest dates back to 1933 when it was invented by Norwegian maverick Hendrik Brun, who used it as a practical undergarment by fusing two fishnets together. The large holes in the mesh trap air, providing insulation against both hot and cold weather. Its popularity peaked in the 1950's but changes in fashion and other materials led to the decline. The other item was nylon shirts – nylon was invented in 1935 and became a product that was widely used from toothbrush tufts, nylon stockings to shirts. Today we tend to get a mixture of polyester and cotton but believe me a 100% nylon shirt was a monster. They were ideal at the time because you could put them in a basic washing machine, hang them up 'drip dry', and wear – not even needing ironing. At school I had to wear a tie all day, in the summer when you sweated (or perspired, a more polite term) the nylon didn't absorb the sweat, neither did nylon 'breathe' so you just melted away in a sticky shirt. The collar would chafe your neck under the school tie and create a rash, and finally, with a string vest underneath for so said insulation again heat – that was completely bonkers. The string vest was OK in winter with normal garments but forget the nylon shirt please!

We hadn't been there long before Cheryl announced that she was marrying Malcolm Jones and wedding preparations began. I became very excited as I wanted to move down into the bedroom she had but then a bombshell hit. My grandmother was going to come and live with us and that was going to be her room, bugger!

Marling School photo, with the horrendous nylon shirt and tie chafing my neck

About 4 weeks before the wedding dad was made redundant from Sperry Gyroscopes and my sister said she would call off the wedding as my parents wouldn't be able to afford all the expenses they had agreed too. But dad would not back down so the wedding went ahead as planned. He now had to find another job.

He was still in contact with several of the former apprentices that he trained at Daniels and one came to his rescue. Lionel Hall was one of the maintenance fitters at BP Plastics (which had taken over the Erinoid site at Lightpill), they had a vacancy, so dad went for it and got it. The upside was he was in his element again getting hands on and what he knew best, the downside was he would be working shifts. There were several other ex-apprentices there and he got a fair amount of leg pulling and pranks played on him in retaliation for when he was their supervisor at Daniels. They would nail his lunch box to the work bench, drill a hole in the bottom of his tea mug, glue his work boots to the floor and when he collected a pack of eggs from one of them when he went to crack them open for Sunday breakfast they were all hard boiled, but he took it all in his stride and made a few inroads too. They had a rest room with a table and hard chairs; he brought in a comfortable rocking chair for himself and harking back to his days at Daniels he wore his brown smock whereas all the others were in overalls.

I would remember being woken by him coming home at 6.00am on a summer day and going to do some gardening before we all got up, he would be whistling away in his happy place – right underneath my bedroom window.

In the winter when he arrived home at 6.00am he would make a huge pan of porridge, just right for a growing schoolboy who then had to walk from Chandos Road to Downfield Road and back for school. A 3-mile round trip down a busy Bath Road and through Strachan's Mill at Lodgemore. If I had enough time, I used to stop by the open mill doors and watch the 'spinning jenny's' going backwards and forwards and the shuttle flying between the threads. I remember the smell from the dyeing area and steam rising from exposed pipes, techniques 100's of years old.

If it was a particularly wet morning I would take the bus from Lightpill, at the bus stop adjacent to Erinoid's at Lightpill Mill. Now for a bit of a history lesson. Plastic was first developed in the mid-19th century from cellulose nitrate The second development was Casein hardened with formaldehyde and patented in Britain in 1911. Casein plastic was made under the trade name "Erinoid" at Lightpill Mills in Stroud for about 70 years from 1912. Unlike the later plastics such as Bakelite, Casein plastic could be dyed in many bright colours. It could withstand the rigours of washing and ironing, dry cleaning solvents, etc. and became popular for buttons and other household goods. It was eventually replaced by oil-based plastics for most uses.

An open sided shed was in the yard nearest the bus stop and the smell from it was overpowering, it contained huge tanks of formaldehyde. If you wanted to see the tanks you would have needed to scale the surrounding wall, which was impossible – set into the concrete top were pieces of sharp glass from broken bottles, etc. a deterrent before razor wire became popular. I only ever saw the tanks when my father sneaked me into the factory for a visit. In later years the site still made plastics the modern way from petrochemicals – first as Mobil and then BP Plastics. Now closed there is still a link to formaldehyde on the site. The far end of Erinoid's cricket pitch at Dudbridge is now under the ownership of Damien Hirst, and his premises on the site are where he made some of his more unusual artwork pieces - death is a central theme in his works. He became famous for a series of artworks in which dead animals (including a shark, a sheep, and a cow) are preserved, sometimes having been dissected, in formaldehyde. History lesson over!

My father didn't get on that well with my grandmother, and they would be almost constantly bickering at one another, she had some strange habits too. She was terrified of thunderstorms and would cover the mirrors (why?) and hide under her quilt until it finished. My father would wind her up by going out into the garden with the poker and holding it up in the air would shout, "come and get me!". Around the early 80's he was to regret that:

During a violent thunderstorm the house received a direct lightning hit. The chimney was destroyed along with half of the roof. The gas fire (which had replaced the oil fire) had jumped 6" into the grate and they had no electric, water or telephone. The fire brigade were called as beams in the roof were smouldering and they put a tarpaulin over the roof. I and my new wife were fast asleep across the valley in Cashes Green oblivious to all this. Dad had got his come uppance from gran!

The morning of Cheryl's wedding, mum and the bridesmaids leaving our new home

Walking home from school one afternoon I met my new brother-in-law, Malcolm, fishing in the canal at Lodgemore. He told me some very exciting news – my father had won on the football pools, the nearest thing to winning the lottery in those days. I ran the rest of the way home to see how rich we were, but not that rich, I think a few £100's but we still went out for a 'slap up meal' at the Hawthorn's restaurant in Amberley to celebrate. My mother drank Dubonnet and lemonade and had a prawn cocktail. I recall, we all had steak!

Holidays were still taken in the 2-week factory shutdown, and we went to various seaside resorts. Tenby, Bournemouth, Gorran Haven, Hollywell Bay, Falmouth and then, when I was 14, a new adventure. We were going up in a plane and flying to Guernsey! We went from Southampton airport in an ancient Bristol Freighter, a car carrying twin engine monster.

It had been sitting on the ground all night during heavy rain and when we took off water that had collected by the skylight (this was a non-pressurised plane) gushed down into my father's lap, he was not amused to say the least. The island was small and quite agricultural, and we had B&B at a farmhouse where they grew tomatoes. Every day we would take one of the many buses to tour different parts of the island and to swim at many of the fine beaches, where I nearly drowned, for the first time, I nearly drowned in the gravel pit at South Cerney a few years later!

What happened? I took a pedalo out from the beach and decided to jump off it into shallow water, I could clearly see the bottom and fish were swimming beneath me, but it wasn't shallow at all. I couldn't swim and went straight down and on surfacing the pedalo was slowly drifting away from me. In a panic I somehow managed to doggy paddle to it and pulled myself back onboard, a very close call – I didn't tell my parents!

Bristol Freighter, about 3 cars and 20 or so passengers
(Photo: Gloucestershire Transport History)

Paul Morse was a school friend from Larksfield Road, I would be up in my bedroom early in the evening when it was getting dark and listen for a whistle outside in the street. That was my signal to go out. Paul would be standing beneath the streetlight just out of sight of the house waiting in Heather Close, we would then spend half an hour or so having a chat and a couple of cigarettes!

In those early days it was permissible, almost mandatory, for Scouts to carry a sheath knife. Mine was a Taylor's Eye Witness with a stag bone handle and compass in the end, passed to me from my father, the one he held as a Rover Scout back in the 1930's.

My Taylor's Eye Witness sheath knife, passed down by my father

Not satisfied with one knife I went into a shop in Fort William when I was about 14 years old, with my parents on holiday with Beavis coach tours in Scotland – on my own I was able to buy a 9" sheath knife! Can you imagine these things happening now?

Eric Daniels could be stubborn as well as a little eccentric, but John had a way with him which forged a great relationship and usually ending with John getting his own way. The first occasion was planning for our very first Scout camp. Eric had the old equipment stored in the stables, so John pulled it all out to prepare for camp. To his amazement the tents appeared to be almost pre-war and motheaten and mouldy. The rest of the equipment wasn't much better. John told him that we needed new kit, Eric stumped up the funds and off John went to buy us some new tents, cooking gear, etc.

Uncle Eric was the group Scout leader and stored all the green ridge tents and the one bell tent in his stable. He always dressed in khaki shorts and top with a green lanyard, even when the uniform changed, he didn't update his. Stephen Marks

I don't know whether you remember but when we went to camp you had tent kits labelled A, B, C etc. That was because Rodborough used to be Sea Scouts, messing about in the small lake/pond at Stringers Court. Uncle Eric, and John, asked me to sort out all the camping kit in one of the outbuildings at Stringers. I found a big box of Naval signalling flags so used these to mark the kit. One big mistake this young leader made was to seal up pegs for tents in plastic bags. Big mistake, they all rotted and I think Uncle Eric paid to replace them. Stuart Leach

What John may have lacked in Scoutmaster knowledge he made up for with his enthusiasm, and to help him he brought in a Scout from Randwick, Stuart Leach. Stuart taught us skills which gave a lot of enjoyment and was always providing us with encouragement when things got tough. One I remember well was the building of the aerial runways through the wood by the Scout hut. Very complicated and lots of knots and lashings but the result always provided a good evening's entertainment in the summer evenings.

Our dad used to work a Sperry Gyroscope in Stonehouse, opposite the Hoffmans factory as a storeman. John Marks worked there. I'm not sure in what capacity but he had to go to the stores to do stock checking. They obviously talked to one another, and John said he needed help with the Rodborough Scouts. I don't think he had a Scouting background but got involved through his two boys. Our Dad said I'd help him, then told me later I was helping him! By then Uncle Eric was getting a bit doddery so John and I ran the Scouts, a Patrol leader on Friday, a very young Scout master on a Monday (I think?). I'd cycle to Scouts which was drag as there was a lot of uphill, then very regularly back to John's house after Scouts for some supper the 10 o'clock news then cycle back to Cashes Green. I'm pretty sure no lights. I think I was allowed special permission by the District Commissioner to have two name tabs on my uniform. Stuart Leach

The first camp was only 4 or 5 days in the far away village of Nupend! We pitched two tents as there were still only a handful of us and lit a fire. John brought a very weird contraption which he placed into and next to the fire – what on earth was it, I wondered? A coil of copper tubing sat in the base of the fire and a tank resembling an oil drum was attached to them filled with water – it was a water heater, genius! That afternoon several of us walked up the road to the Off Licence and bought bottles of cider – something else which would never happen today. On the Sunday we were visited by John's wife Joan (more about Joan later) who brought us roast chicken and veg from home, no campfire lunch that day.

I remember Nupend. The paddock was where I camped for either a second or first class hike. Anyway, Uncle Eric brought a friend with him, Mr Syms. They sat regally in a tent and chatted away. Mr Syms had a strange device with him, a little tin with holes in it and a small handle. I watched with fascination as he used this tea infuser, I'd never seen one before. Stuart Leach John also brought in a Territorial Army Sergeant Major, Dick Keithley. Dick taught us drill and how to be as smart as possible in our uniforms, along with map reading, survival and tracking skills. Between them Stuart and Dick provided us with a solid background to good Scouting, many of those skills I can still use even now.

Proficiency badges were always a big thing in Scouting. The normal ones were not that difficult – First Aider, Cyclist, Cook and Map reader but others were a little trickier. My love of aircraft led me to gain my Air Spotters badge, but nothing had prepared me for my Backwoods badge! Being delivered at the Cranham Scout Centre I was ushered across the road and deep into the wood, where I and my fellow Scouts, were met by Brian Pegler and Keith Stanley, two Scout leaders from Randwick. First task – build a bivouac, but what with? Down by the stream there were plenty of giant rhubarb leaves so with my trusty sheath knife I cut a large arm full and dragged them back into the wood. Next cutting some small branches, with the knife once more, I proceeded to make a framework against a tree and wove the leaves into it. Pretty nifty stuff for a 14-year-old I thought. Finally cutting some fibres out of wood to make twine I tied it all together – result!

Next, down to a clearing where we made fires and given a fish to gut and cook. Here we hit a problem as I hated fish, the smell, and the taste. Still to this day. So, please sir, can I have something else? At which point I was given a rabbit! We proceeded to cook our meal and were tasked to boil water in a brown paper bag. I won't go into technicalities, but it is possible. At this point I must have done something wrong or maybe got a bit lippy, I was strung upside down by my feet from a tree for 10 minutes as punishment. Overnight it rained heavily but success, I was still dry in the morning, Backwoods badge awarded and off home.

The summer of 1967 was memorable for the county camp at Miserden Park, which was attended by the then Chief Scout Sir Charles MacLean. The event was a complete washout with mud up to the knees. Our cub pack carried out a visit and I went along to help. We slithered down the grassy banks and traipsed around in mud and torrential rain, not a lot of fun that day, but I met up with some Scouts from Randwick and friendships were made that have lasted.

In 1968 it was camp planning time and John, Eric, a couple of others and I piled into Eric's Ford Cortina estate – we didn't like his driving, so John helped himself to the driver's seat.

Uncle Eric was dangerous in that car. He used to ferry Scouts around and was either short sighted or colour blind because at the traffic lights in Cainscross (the old ones) he'd ask the Scouts what colour the lights were. I'm sure Roger Griffin convinced him on one occasion that red was green, and they blithely sailed through, without mishap so he could tell the tale with a great degree of relish afterwards. Stuart Leach

The day was spent looking for a suitable site in Monmouthshire and finally we found one on the river Monnow at Rockfield. Our site was opposite the Rockfield Recording Studios which over time saw great musicians pass through. Oasis, Iggy Pop, Nigel Kennedy, Simple Minds, Coldplay, Black Sabbath and even Queen, who recorded "Bohemian Rhapsody" there. On our way home we stopped at Skenfrith and clambered around on the castle battlements for a happy hour while Eric and John had lunch. Later that summer we travelled back to Rockfield, this time on the back, yes on the back, of an open lorry.

The kit was loaded and we all climbed on top of It, we also brought a ships bell that Eric had tucked away in the coach house and rang it like mad as we drove through villages and towns on the way. Oh, by the way, no seat belts sitting on the back of an open lorry – whatever were we thinking about!

At Rockfield there are two instances I remember. The bank of the river was sandy, and you Scouts carved your names in the bank. Inevitably one person was injured and came for help. I put my thumb over the wound to stop the blood while the first aid kit was found but could not understand why he was still bleeding. The knife had gone right through. John had to take him to hospital. The second incident was my "O" level exam results were due. Our dad had been to school, copied down the results from the window where they were published, got in touch somehow with the landlord at Rockfield who then brought them to the site. It seems everybody knew my results before I did! I remember sun every day and just a great time. Stuart Leach

Never to shirk away from a challenge we decided to do a night hike, around the Rockfield area. One of the younger Scouts developed a blister and I ended up giving him a piggyback for the last 2 miles or so.

Rockfield camp, 1968. I am 5th from left. Last three on right are Uncle Eric, Stuart Leach and John Marks. (Credit: Bristol Evening News)

On our last night there, we met with Girl Guides from Pontllanfraith and Blackwood who were camping a few fields away. We built a campfire, brought out our campfire blankets and entertained the guides with songs and jacket potatoes from the fire. I ended up writing to one of them for a couple of weeks afterwards – deja-vu, could have ended in a similar situation to my parents!

I am in the centre, cooking outside Rodborough Tabernacle, circa. 1968.

Early in 1968 the District offered two places at the Cotswold Gliding Club, Aston Down for Scouts. Interviews for the successful candidate took place at Randwick HQ. I applied, due to my love of aircraft, and was successful, the other one was Chris Wakefield a Scout from Amberley. I had a bicycle, but Chris had a Lambretta scooter. I would cycle to his house in Woodchester and he would take us to the gliding club most weekends. In return for helping on the ground we would get a free lesson. These eventually became shorter as work on the ground became busier, and sadly we discontinued the project.

Approaching 16 years of age I decided I wanted a Lambretta and constantly pestered Chris to let me have a go on his around the perimeter track at the airfield, and he eventually gave in. Unfortunately, I knew very little about clutch control and throttle co-ordination and promptly fell off on a bend changing gear. He wouldn't let me ride it again!

Campfires and girls cropped up again in November 1968 when Uncle Eric held a bonfire party in his garden and invited the Rodborough Guides. Many I knew from either primary school days or living locally, except for a well-spoken blonde girl from the far side of Rodborough Common who I didn't know. I was 15 years old and totally smitten, wanted to sit and talk to her all evening and finally as the evening ended, I did something very brave – I asked her out for the following evening, and foolishly she agreed! After the bonfire I walked home with Judith Kemp and quizzed her mercilessly about this newfound friend that I was about to meet again.

The Rover Hut was not used on a Sunday evening so Chris Marks, the blonde girl (Jo-Anne Lusty) and I would sneak in there, light a fire, bring in a few beers and food and chill out (if that was a saying in 1969) before another week at school or work. My grandmother had an old valve radio which we took and rigged up an aerial on the roof. It had programmes such as The Light Programme and Hilversum, but we found Radio Luxembourg!

One Friday evening, in the early summer of 1969 I turned up at Scouts to be informed by John that Nick Sutton, Chris Marks and I were going to compete in the Gloucestershire County Challenge Hike – the next day! After profuse complaining, which never worked, he told us that our parents had been contacted already and our kit was being packed, he was collecting us at 7.00am on Saturday morning.

We were dropped off at the Scout hut in Tuffley and a minibus took us to somewhere near Raglan, Monmouthshire. Here we were dropped. More disconcerting was that most, if not all, the other teams were Venture Scouts (In 1967, as part of the adoption of The Chief Scouts' Advance Party Report, Venture Scouts replaced the Rover Scouts and Senior Scout programs in The Scout Association, Cub Scouts replaced Wolf Cubs). We were by far the youngest. With a map reference for our overnight stop, and a reference for the finish we set off, map and compass in hand, to cross into the lower reaches of the Black Mountain range. We reached the overnight stop in good time and broke open our rations that John and Dick had provided for us, they were really good. I noticed a pub up the road so bought cider, yet again.

The following day we had our ration pack porridge oats, which we had soaked overnight, filled our water bottles, and headed off. After about an hour the cloud came down and we couldn't see our hands in front of our faces. We had two choices, carry on hoping to break through it and re-establish our surroundings or head back to the overnight stop to be picked up. After the good training we had from Dick, we decided to go on and by a stroke of luck we noticed the top of three radio masts poking through the cloud in the far distance and managed to work out exactly where we were. Apparently, most teams turned back but we were the 2nd team to reach the finish. I can't remember how many miles we had to cover but probably around 30 or so. A fantastic achievement and one that we were all proud of, especially as we had beaten most of the older ones! My time in Scouts was memorable, as no doubt you will have noticed, John was impressed by my commitment (or confused by it) and made me troop leader, a recognition I didn't come across in many other troops.

When I was growing up, if you wanted to see a friend, you'd walk or bike round to their house and knock on their door. If they weren't in, you'd just have to go back home again. None of this mobile phone lark! John Chenery

At Marling we were allocated a 'tutor', a sort of mentor for helping our progression through the years and even career planning. Mine was 'Jimmy' Nicklin who lived in Rodborough Avenue, one of only a few teachers I actually liked. I told him that I wanted to become an RAF dog handler, as I recalled my visit to the open evening at the Technical College when I was younger. He didn't think that was a good idea as he felt there would be no promotion prospects from lower ranks, Marling school pupils were expected to be officer material!

Towards the beginning of 1968 I had two things occupying my mind, Jo-Anne Lusty and pending GCE examinations. I would meet Jo-Anne from High School and walk with her all the way up to the Prince Albert before saying goodbye and then back down Walkley Hill and home. Only to do the trip up to her house opposite the fort in the evenings. We would walk on the common and at weekends descend into Stroud for illegal drinking in The Post Office pub cellar bar, frequented by many other Marling and High School pupils, and not even 16 years old! The police would come in now and again, but we were wise and put our alcoholic drinks under the table and instead had a reserve bottle of coke, etc. to put in its place.

We did mock examinations in the winter in preparation for our forthcoming GCE's. I was sitting English, Maths, History, Geography, Chemistry, Physics, Woodwork and Geometrical & Technical Drawing – phew, that was plenty. My problem though was that I was much more interested in Jo-Anne than I was in studying, whereas she was an ideal student and would work hard revising. Subsequently my exam results and career path didn't go to plan!

Early in the spring of 1969 I was called into my grammar school tutor's office. He had some bad news, I had applied to join the Fleet Air Arm (FAA) and was hoping to become a navigator/observer in Buccaneer's, Gannet's or Sea Vixen's, however a change in defence policy stated that the FAA was going to concentrate on helicopter pilots and crew so I would have to change my plan. I certainly did change it; no way was I going to go up in a helicopter – I didn't trust them one bit! So, I went home that afternoon distraught, 3 months away from my GCE exams and no future. When I got home there was a green van parked outside and a man in dirty overalls, flat cap and wearing a leather safety belt up the pole opposite. Another engineer was on the ground watching him. Noticing that I looked upset, the engineer asked me why, so I told him. 'Why not join the GPO and become a telephone engineer?' he said, he turned out to be Peter White who was the Stroud engineering union branch officer. So, this was exactly what I did.

Prior to even receiving my GCE results I was called to the Technical College in Brunswick Road, Gloucester to sit the GPO entrance exams, along with, believe it or not, another six pupils from my school as well. I passed, some of the other five hadn't! A few weeks later I went to Bearlands House in Gloucester for an interview – another pass! Later still I collected a tool wallet and some tools, bib and brace overalls, wellington boots, paramatta raincoat, sou'wester hat and a very heavy but warm GPO labelled overcoat – I was ready to go – almost. Just a holiday in the USA with my parents then off to work at the beginning of August.

Approaching my 16th birthday I decided I wanted to buy a scooter, a Lambretta Li125 to be exact, my father was a big motorcycle fan so he wasn't impressed.

SIXTEEN!

I had to ask permission to leave school before the very end of term to allow me to go to America, so I was summoned to the headmaster's study for a final meeting. I thought it would be amusing to wear a blue shirt and my Technical School tie on the last day and marched into his office. However, he was not amused. He told me to go, saying, "Rebellious to the end Wilkins, rebellious to the end, get out!". I was free at last.

Having ridden the scooter for about 3 days I decided to ride up through Kingscourt, up Bowl Hill and onto the common, but in Bowl Hill I rode straight into the front of an oncoming car – oops! I flew over the bonnet and hurt my leg and knee, the side of the scooter was crumpled and the car had a dent in the wing. 'Just you wait until your father gets home' was no doubt going to be said, and he was not happy. He agreed to pay for the damage to the car and my mother banned me from riding it until we came back from America.

My after accident, stripped down, Lambretta. I kept it like this, it looked cool!

Off I flew from Heathrow to Philadelphia with my parents and grandmother to visit our American cousins. While there we had a massive BBQ while watching the first moon landing. This was during a violent thunderstorm in Newark, New Jersey – my cousin pulled the BBQ into his garage – we could have died from CO poisoning.

I went in the first car I had seen with air conditioning, rode a horse on my other cousin's ranch, went to a drive-in movie, saw a live baseball game, had a demonstration of a microwave cooker, went to a shopping mall, cleaned my cousin's gun arsenal, watched colour multi-channel TV and saw hummingbirds.

We went to Washington and visited the grave of President Kennedy in Arlington Cemetery and I climbed the 900+ steps up inside the Washington Monument, all 555 feet of it. The day was hot and very humid and by the time I reached the top I was bathed in perspiration, but the view was awesome.

Root beer was new to me, it is a carbonated beverage traditionally flavoured with the bark and roots of various plants, such as sassafras or sarsaparilla, along with other herbs like wintergreen, vanilla, and licorice root. I sat out on the 'stoop' one evening as night fell rocking backwards and forwards in the chair and sneaked a few bottles of it out of the fridge. Having finished the 3rd bottle I started to see flashes of light in front of my eyes, drunk already?

I rushed inside and announced that I had drunk too much and was seeing flashes before my eyes, my cousin burst out laughing. Root beer was non-alcoholic, and the flashes were fireflies! Thes insects would rise up from the long grass then ignite their glow going skywards – a truly amazing sight for a 16-year-old.

Our Pan-Am Boeing 707 at Philadelphia

Kennedy's grave – in need of some weeding

My cousins ranch house, Circle Star Farm near Harrisburg (PA)

July 4th, not a day we remember in the UK, but they certainly do in America! It was 'party time' at the Circle Star Farm. Tables were laid out in the yard and the whole Brougher family turned up. We were allowed to join them as temporary Americans for the day.

Independence Day celebrations about to kick off

My cousin made reproduction Red Indian costumes, I made a good model

On arrival back home my results had arrived, a good choice too as the only GCE passes I obtained were in Geography, Geometrical and Technical Drawing, Physics and Chemistry. A complete failure for entry into the FAA, I didn't even get Maths and English!

It all really started in 1973 when I rode the staggering distance to Pitchcombe and back from Rodborough Common where I lived . Very soon we were riding to Gloucester, Cheltenham and Cirencester when we got the `bug` and soon set our sights on The Severn Bridge & Chepstow…. To be a stunning 55-mile return trip around 1975.

For me, growing up on Rodborough Common my daily rides involved either Rodborough, Walkley or possibly Cowcombe hills just to get home and hence my climbing skills were honed. With a few of local mates – Rob Deane; Mark Hollies; Martin Baxter and Paul Salmon we would often race up Rodborough Hill and the last one up would buy the beer at the pub at the top – namely the Prince Albert. Most of us were nudging 6' by then so getting served wasn't an issue !! I remember a silly evening trying to get up Blackness in Thrupp, to no avail since the pedals stopped turning about 25' up due to the 1:4 gradient.

The bright lights of Chepstow had beckoned, so we figured the next obvious extension to our ride would be to loop back up to Gloucester on the west side of the Severn. My naïve assumption was that from Chepstow to Glawster would be flattish since it followed the River. How wrong can you be ! The hills up through Lydney, Blakeney and Newnham were brutal and soul destroying but we succeeded and afterwards even started to add Cirencester in the River loop to give us the long-sought 100-mile epic.

Once we were routinely riding 100 miles daily, the sky (or our legs) was the limit – we did Oxford and back, Basingstoke return and the river loop ended up as Stroud; Cirencester; Chippenham; Bath; Bristol; Chepstow; Gloucester; Cheltenham and back to Stroud. We were nudging 150 miles a day by around early 76 until one day our mate John Samuel announced his 165-mile day epic the previous weekend ! At this point the gauntlet had been thrown down, so Mark Hollies and I decided a London return should break the 200-mile threshold. Setting out in the school summer holiday of 1976, at 16 years of age, I rose at 5am and met Mark at Aston Down. Onwards through Cirencester; Oxford; High Wycombe; Uxbridge to Acton and finally Hammersmith

Odeon (the A40 then wasn't very bike friendly so' twas a bit of an ordeal). We got to Hammersmith around 11am and downed a pint of gold top milk before turning right around and went back the same way. I can't recall much of the return ride, but I do remember parting company with him at Aston Down in the dark and struggling to even turn the pedals back home where I arrived at 9.30pm. I slept the entire next day !!

Once we left Marling in '77, we decided to ride to the Swiss Alps – namely Interlaken, Wilderswil and Lauterbrunnen. Accompanied by Martin Baxter and Paul Salmon it was a 5-day ride, sleeping in corn fields; abandoned boats and once in the Alps we frequently camped rough in the forests. Our diet was sardines n rice; Ravioli; Spam; Alpen and apples that we nicked from roadside orchards. I recall the entire one-month ride cost a staggering 60 quid, and we resembled feral animals once we got home in time to see the A level results posted on the headmaster's window at school. Bikes are still a great part of me, and I'm proud that both our sons now in their 20's have become passionate bike guys and our youngest is likely to become a bike R&D engineer when he graduates university here in the States next Spring. It was a fantastic way to live in and explore the Stroud Valleys and Cotswolds. How grateful I am to have had the opportunity. *Simon Hunter, ex-Rodborough, now living in Gainesville, Florida and working as a 'Heavy Check Technical Representative' for a US airline specialising in Airbus and Embraer jet aircraft*

Simon and his companions in the Alps near Zermatt – camping in the woods eating sardines n rice no doubt! (Photo credit: Simon Hunter)

Although Halfords was good for some money I was already thinking about another scooter and even more, so I took a job in the few weeks until I started with the GPO. BP Plastics were moving their warehouse facility at Thrupp to newer and larger premises in Gloucester, myself and a few other 16-year-olds were recruited to clear the warehouses of all the plastics and rubbish to clear the old site. We got paid really well and I decided to treat both my parents to a meal in the Imperial Hotel to celebrate the end of the project. During the meal the fire siren went off on top of Hill Paul building, used to raise the on-call firemen, must have been a big fire. It was a big fire, a warehouse in Gloucester full of plastic was burning down, fire appliances were flooding into Gloucester!

The years moved on and Grampy Cook passed and Auntie Lottie was living at Stalcot on her own. My mate Rog. and I were into all things musical… well it was now the sixties, we were into guitars, girls and guzzling! So, I moved into Lottie's spare room which we called the 'Den' and Roger Hill and I played our electric guitars as loudly as possible as Lottie liked the company and Mum and Dad knew where I was? Girls came and went and Roger and I took to visiting the Princess Royal pub taproom, up Tabernacle Walk over the 'Cockpits', down the acre on the right. We were underage but Reg. and Olga were happy to take pennies for pints and so, the life of two would be rockstars had begun. Oh NO! John Cook, Rodborough

John (standing) and Roger with their guitars before descending on the Princess Royal

Only a week to go before starting my own apprenticeship and I felt unwell, in a matter of hours I was feeling really very unwell. I told my grandmother then went to bed and when my mother arrived home, I was already in the first stages of Glandular Fever. This lasted for 3 weeks, and I can't remember much of that time apart from a raging fever, no appetite and constant sleeping. The fever eventually broke, and I awoke one morning to say I really would like some toast for breakfast, but it was still several weeks before I was fit to start work and I missed the initial stages of my apprenticeship.

I also missed the Apprentice 'A' training course at Shirehampton, Bristol. Instead, I was thrown to the wolves in mid–September – told to report to Brian Hale, the jointer at Stroud, at a location just off the town centre, in a manhole in the middle of Merrywalks roundabout outside the Police Station.

Brian had two other engineers on his shift and as I parked my Lambretta on the grass verge opposite I heard voices coming from the back of a green GPO lorry, but I couldn't see inside as a tarpaulin was draped across the open doorway – should I go in? I moved the tarpaulin aside and was amazed at what I saw, the back of the lorry had a makeshift table and chairs and a kettle boiling away on a gas ring placed on the floor. The air was grey with tobacco smoke. The seven-thirty tea break apparently – rituals I needed to adapt to quickly.

After the introductions the inevitable happened, "Maf, pop up the tobacconist and get 20 Capstan and 20 Senior Service, then on the way back stop at the bakers and get 4 lardy cakes", so off I went on my first trip of the day. The second trip was a bit strange; the local engineering depot was not far away in Lansdown, and Brian asked me to go to the stores there to get a 'long weight'. Naïve as ever off I trotted and soon entered the stores where I placed my request. The storeman gave me a nice smile and told me to go and sit in the signing-on room, which I did. After what seemed like hours someone came and told me the truth – strike one to the GPO humour, nil to the apprentice!

'God's Poor Orphans' (GPO) was a term used many times and my first week pay packet was in cash, £5,17 shillings and 6d. However, I could give my mother housekeeping out of that, put fuel in my scooter, buy 'fags' and go down the pub. I also retained my Saturday job in Halfords until finishing my apprenticeship, getting a hefty 25% discount too on tools and spare parts for the car I bought later – happy days indeed.

There were quite a few scooter friends in Stroud and we would congregate in Stratford Park evenings and on Sunday afternoons. Racing up and down the gravel drive as it was then we would create big plumes of dust, then a guy (who was some sort of park manager) would rush over and tell us basically to," fxxk off", which we did then came back about 30 minutes later. The girls were there too in their Crombie jackets and tonic trousers, me in my white trainers and jeans with turn-ups, and the obligatory Ben Sherman short sleeved shirt!

When we got bored we would line up in Stratford Road then race to the bottom of Paganhill Lane and return, seeing who was the quickest. On the Sunday's we would take whichever girl needed a lift and go into Stroud for the Gaumont cinema evening film – two which spring to mind were Soldier Blue and Emmanuel, very weird!

At the same time, I was still going to chapel every Sunday, my mother had recruited me for the choir when I was eleven and I was still singing there at sixteen, but not really sure why I bothered as I was by no means religious, I just didn't want to upset her. I would get to the chapel early as my first task was to put all the hymn numbers and order of service announcements in place, before sitting with the choir at 11.00am and listening to every boring sermon. When it finished though I would jump on my scooter and head off to the Kings Head in Kingscourt, have a couple of Brewmaster's, a packet of crisps and a smoke and then home for Sunday lunch. I stopped going to church a few months later, my mother didn't say a word about it. Also, I should have had free drinks as my great, great grandmother used to be the landlady there!

Then it happened, I had to go for my Apprentice 'A' training course at Shirehampton, a rail warrant was presented, and on a warm Monday morning I stood at Stonehouse station waiting for a train to take me to Bristol Temple Meads. On my own I had never been further than Cheltenham, and that was for the dreaded Monday technical college classes.

At Temple Meads I looked for the bus to Shirehampton, but not a bus in sight, I waited and waited until I was told, "Bus drivers are on strike". I decided to walk with my suitcase with no idea how far the RETC was from the station *(it apparently is 6 miles and would take me over 2 hours)*.

After a few miles my arms ached, and I was sweating profusely, I also had no idea where I was! Then a car pulled up with two young men in it and they offered me a lift, for which I was truly grateful, they even took me right to the gates of the training school. I walked into the office to register and mentioned the difficulty I experienced getting to Shirehampton, the receptionist laughed, "you should have rung us, we would have sent our minibus for you!". Next, I was given an address for my 'digs' which was just down the road and on arriving there I was met by a very attractive middle age blond woman, who showed me to my room – which I was sharing with two other apprentices and a faultsman jointer, no en-suite either. She then showed us her door, which had a Yale lock on it, not surprising I suppose as she was quite a looker.

Early morning in the garden with our first cat Lucky, I am now earning real money so I am lucky too!

Even though only I was only just 16 years old myself and the other apprentices would descend on the George Inn pub on Shirehampton Green after dinner, on returning to the 'digs' we always found a huge plate of ham sandwiches and flasks of coffee on the dining room table – the room we shared was a bit off but the meals and food she gave us was excellent.

On the second week I ventured to the local post office and saw a girl behind the counter who I took a shine too. After a couple more visits I asked her if she would like me to take her for a drink one evening and she accepted. She lived in Avonmouth so I walked her home afterwards and just before her house she pulled me into a dark alley and made a proposition, still naïve I declined and sprinted back the way I had come, didn't go back to the post office again either.

Towards the end of the course one of our instructors, Ray Whiting, asked us if we fancied a trip to a strip club, no refusals, so he arranged transport for us all to go to Cleopatras in Easter Compton. This was going to be another new experience for me and out came a woman with a massive snake around her neck. I had never seen a naked woman, was very naïve and I don't like snakes. I was a little embarrassed, so I moved towards the back of the room, to continue watching and was standing next to a 'slot machine', it sold Castella cigars. I put my two shillings in and pulled the drawer at the bottom to take my cigar, being a smoker like many kids of my age in those days, then pushed the drawer back in. As you always did, I attempted to open the drawer once more – just in case. It opened and out popped another cigar. I continued this until I had filled all my pockets with Castella's, then shared them out with the others when we returned to Shirehampton.

The apprentice 'A' course line up. I am 4th from the right in the back row

There was no Venture Scout Unit at Rodborough, but there was a large Cub Scout group now being led by Joan Marks, 'Akela', John's wife. She was helped by Assistant Cub Scout Leader Janet Gardiner and another Senior Scout from Randwick, Andrew (Haggis) Leach, the older brother of Stuart. John and Joan encouraged me to become an Assistant cub scout leader and this is where I spent probably the next 5 years. As the pack grew, we had help from another Randwick Venture Scout, Dave Richards and then Len Scarrott.

Haggis, as he was known throughout his life, had a Ford Popular. The sit up and beg type. After Cubs, Janet, Haggis and I would pile into the car and head to Joan's for supper. Two things transpired from this. The front seat fell through the floorpan and I ended up sitting in the footwell, bonus though was that I had a new girlfriend again, Janet, thanks to Joan and John!

Cubs met inside the main hall within the Tabernacle which had plenty of space and light to do cub Scout things, unlike the damp Rover Hut. Sadly, they never played British Bulldogs!

Being a teenager was hard work in itself. A constant stream of girlfriends, holidays abroad, scouting, making new friends and fitting in some work alongside.

I seemed to have a knack for changing girlfriends regularly, most lasted a few months, some just days. Part of this was down to my mother who was now also working at BP Plastics, the PA to the General Manager. A lot of young girls worked there, and my mother would somehow fix me up with one every now and again, I think she may have been positioning herself for a nice daughter-in-law, it wasn't going to happen! I don't think I was serious enough as a teenager to have a steady girlfriend as there were much too many other things to enjoy.

A time of great change and opportunities – look out world, here I come!

A regular income enabled me to buy this Lambretta TV200 from Roger Savage, Eira's brother

Coach holiday with my parents and relatives in Berwang, Austria

In the summer holidays I did some occasional work with Beavis coaches. Painting or cleaning around the office or washing and cleaning the coaches, apart from a small pay packet I also had the chance to go on a coach holiday abroad if they had any empty spaces, which fell in nicely when I was 18 and went to Austria and Switzerland once more.

Austria with Beavis coach tours again, checking my wallet I believe, my mother getting her gateau on the right. This was the last with my parents, on my own for the next one, I had money!

Approaching 17 I was still going out with Janet Gardner, and I bought a car. It was my brother-in-laws Mini and I paid £50 for it. As soon as I hit 17, I started having lessons, with Janet teaching me as she held a full licence. I would ride down to her house in Cainscross on my scooter, pick her up and go back home for the car. We would then drive out to the Daneway, Bell at Sapperton or even Tunnel House at Coates. Have a few drinks and then reverse the drive back set-up. I also took lessons from Bob Oldmeadow, who was part of the Kingscourt Oldmeadow family and passed on my first attempt. Now Janet didn't have to get on my scooter and mess her hair up any longer!

I was no stranger to driving a car though, when I was about 15 years old my father had an Austin A30 van and an Austin A35 car, he broke the rear differential just outside Minchinhampton and wanted to get the car back home to repair it, but how. Solution, he got a tow rope, bundled me in the car and off to Minchinhampton we went. He put me in the broken car, told me to keep the rope taut at all times and then towed me steering the car all the way back home!

Another time one of my father's work mates (not co-workers then) took me to Aston Down airfield to fly his model plane. He had a Hillman Minx and said I could drive it back home some of the way, who was I to refuse. This time I had an engine and throttle/clutch to master but I did alright and managed the 4 miles to Tom Long's Post without hitting anything.

While I was still learning to drive my father made a strange request, he wanted to borrow my Mini to go on a journey, his old Land Rover was too fuel thirsty and leaked oil like a sieve! Stupidly I agreed then the full story came out, he wanted to go to the Farnborough Air Show. I agreed of course, then the bombshell, he was taking 3 other work colleagues too. Four adults in an 850cc Mini all the way to Farnborough and back with no motorways – I thought that was the last I would ever see of it, but no, he arrived back just before midnight and the Mini was no more worse for wear.

Apprenticeship was now in full swing. Every Monday was 'college' – Day Release. Maths, Engineering Science, Telephony & Telegraphy and General Studies. I hated school and this was no better, remember I didn't even get a GCE in Maths or English. I would drive to Cheltenham from home, about 15 miles, to the North Gloucestershire Technical College. Initially on my Lambretta which was fine in summer but awful in winter.

Another apprentice, Dave Griffiths, would come as my passenger and would often fall asleep on the back on our way there in the morning. Lunch was taken in the Norwood Arms as the food in the college canteen was crap – a couple of pints, a ham roll and crisps then back to college. The end of the day came at around 8.00pm after our Telephony & Telegraphy session, we would be driving home in the dark with a stupid bulb lighting our way, stopping at the Royal William in Cranham for a few more pints, more food and a game of darts!

Prior to Bonfire Night we were heading home followed by another apprentice, Roy Hooper, he was on his motorbike. Dave on the back of my scooter casually smoking a cigarette reached into his pocket and pulled out a 'banger', which he lit with the cigarette end and promptly threw it over his shoulder at Roy – not once but about a dozen times. Roy was good fun and in the 3rd year was one of the District's Apprentice of the Year. Generally, at the presentation carried out by the Telephone Manager recipients would have asked for a book of something telephone oriented, Roy asked for an anvil. When asked why his reply was, 'I want to see the Telephone Manager pick it up to give it to me!'.

My next stint was subscriber maintenance, I was put with Maurice Screen from Randwick who for his patch had the town of Nailsworth and the villages of Uley and Leighterton. He had a GPO green Morris Minor van loaded with stuff I had yet to learn how to use, e.g. line vice, Tester SA9083 in a big leather case and climbing irons to name a few. These were happy days for me, Maurice was a good instructor, and we very quickly jelled. He wore a grey cardigan with deep pockets, his pipe in one and tobacco pouch in the other – so I did the same and we puffed away on our pipes most days. Maurice had one bad trait though, he was almost always late, and the Inspector would have drawn the line in the signing on book before he arrived quite often. I would already have gone to the stores to replenish our van stock, and we would drive off to Nailsworth with a few faults written in his notebook, first stop though – the café next door to the fire station for a bacon sandwich and tea!

One particular subscriber we had to visit regularly nearly made me a vegetarian way back in 1970, Hilliers Bacon Curing Ltd in Newmarket, Nailsworth. A large sprawling site with some ancient buildings and a smell which permeated the air as you approached! With a large switchboard and numerous extension around the site we would go almost weekly, and if my memory is correct I hated going on a Tuesday and Friday – slaughter day. Not only did they make pork products but they slaughtered the pigs too, and occasionally cattle. I won't go into details but the process 55 years ago was pretty basic, the noise and smell awful.

Several departments were pretty gross – the brawn plant (a type of cured meat or meat jelly traditionally made from the head of a pig) and the chitling plant (a food traditionally made from the small intestines of pigs) and I almost threw up as the heads rolled into the plant via a stone chute. 'English pre-packed bacon' was a chilled cutting room where the bacon was cut and put into steel trays ready to go to the many Hilliers shops spread around the county, that wasn't too bad and the exotic smells coming from the herb and spice storeroom was almost hallucinogenic!

On top of all this they made pork pies, steak and kidney pies, sausages – as we used to say, you can eat every part of a pig except his squeak! Maurice had a daily diet of the sandwiches he brought from home plus he would buy a daily steak and kidney pie. The weird thing to me at the time was that he ate it cold, and cut it into chunks with the penknife he used to clean out his pipe, not sure if when he smoked he got a steak flavour or when he ate he got a smoky pie?

Another sad thing is that the Nailsworth valley was crammed with engineering works and factories – to name many I remember and visited starting at Lightpill with Erinoids/Mobil Plastics then Critchcraft, Bentley Pianos, Arthurs Press and Carr Tanning, Henry Workman Saw Mill/Denis Brown timber haulage (Woodchester); Fenworths, Newman Hender, Dunkirk Mills (Inchbrook); Egypt Mill, Chamberlains Mill, Spring Mill and Longford Mill (Nailsworth) and a lot more I have forgotten no doubt.

Maurice would frequent the Vine Tree pub in Randwick and I would go up there some evenings, making more new friends, many from Randwick Scouts that I had met at Miserden in 1967. We became quite close as we would also bump into each other on scouting activities ranging from district camps to helping at Cranham Scout HQ. In my early 20's I left behind the Rodborough Cubs and became Assistant Venture Scout Leader at Randwick. I was friendly with Dave Jefferies who was coincidentally the Venture Scout Leader. Dave and I would meet at The Vine Tree in Randwick, and this is where my friendship with others was re-established. Dave was a Motorway Police Constable who drove his Lotus Elan with gusto. As I was a car freak, we immediately jelled and Dave asked me to help him with the Venture Scout Unit, police shifts making regular meetings difficult for him.

My first memory of doing silly things as a Venture Scout Leader was Dave announcing we would arrange a weekend camp, in February! This was to be in Welsh Bicknor, across the River Wye in the Forest of Dean. Dave, through his strange contacts as a PC, managed to borrow a 7.5-ton lorry from C M Downton of Hardwicke. We filled it with kit, canoes and Venture Scouts and headed off to the Forest on a Friday evening. When we reached Highnam Dave realised we needed diesel. He drove onto the petrol station forecourt and promptly demolished the canopy – oops!

We arrived in a field, erected tents, set a fire and settled down for the night. One thing neither of us appreciated was that many of the Venture Scouts only had thin nylon sleeping bags, unlike our own 3 or 4 season ones. That night we could have lost most of them to frostbite but, fully dressed inside their bags, they survived. The following morning, we attempted to get the gas burner going but it wouldn't, freezing cold gas canisters don't work. That night I slept with the gas cylinder by my feet inside my sleeping bag, the next morning we had flame!

We went to a lake above Llanthony Priory and broke the ice and canoed. Afterwards we walked Offa's Dyke and descended towards the Priory to a pub with a roaring coal fire. We piled in and to our delight they made toasted sandwiches, never seen or heard of before, but we had quite a few. Returning to our frozen camp site, we decided, rather than light the fire, we would go in search of another pub. We found the Dog & Muffler across the river Wye on Joyford Hill, Coleford where we played darts with the locals. I returned to this pub when I moved to the Forest of Dean in 2006, but it didn't seem quite the same.

On my Apprentice 'C' training course at Shirehampton in February 1971 we had relay adjusting to do, and I was quite up to speed with this before going there. I smugly took my adjusted relays up to the instructor, who promptly bent them all and told me to do them again, I wasn't so smug next time. At the time I still had my Mini, which as a theft precaution had a switch under the dashboard to cut off the electrical feed to the fuel pump. Leaving my digs, this time in Sea Mills, no Mini parked outside. A quick look around and there it was about 100 yards down the road with the driver's door open, ground to a halt from fuel starvation. Thief Nil-Melvyn 1. Here Ray Whiting once more said he would organize a night out, but this time to the Bristol Bier Kellar. It appeared that he got a discount for a large party, but we didn't fully make up the numbers, so those that went in first came out the fire exit and joined the back of our queue – result.

Monday February 15th, 1971 was 'D-day', the day of decimalisation when the old pounds, shillings and pence would be made decimal, as it now remains. Queueing to go into the training school canteen that lunchtime the queue was stretching out of the door, the poor woman on the till was in a right panic, she just couldn't get her head around converting all the different prices into decimal currency. Eventually getting to the front of the queue I think I paid 35p for my sausage, egg and chips!

Throughout my apprenticeship I continued every Saturday at Halfords, the heavy discount really helping me with spares for my Mini. Lucy was still there and looking gorgeous but had just got married, so that was out of the question still. Bang opposite was the shoe shop Freeman, Hardy & Willis and they had a pretty blond Saturday girl. I would stand in the doorway of our shop occasionally looking at her, she would often do the same. This continued for weeks but for some really odd reason I never asked her out, can't think for the life of me why not!

One Saturday a scruffy, bearded guy in filthy mud-stained overalls came in and I went to serve him. That was how it used to be done, no hiding, hoping the customer hadn't noticed you like now. He asked me for some carbide, that floored me as I knew almost everything we sold but that was new on me. Carbide apparently is actually calcium carbide which when mixed with water produces acetylene gas. He was in cave rescue and portable acetylene gas lamps, worn on the hat or carried by hand, were widely used in mining in the early twentieth century and they were still employed by cavers. He was adamant that we sold it so off I trotted to the manager – who gave me a key and said it was in the dustbin on the upstairs landing. Very strange to find a padlock on a dustbin and even stranger to see it was filled with sand. Reaching into the sand I found several small tins of powder, the carbide. It must have been some pretty scary stuff to use if it had to be stored that way!

Terry Jones in the newly opened Stroud Automatic Telephone Exchange 1968 (Photo: Dave Jones)

Finally, 'Telephone Exchange Maintenance'. I was to meet two people here who ran Stroud Exchange, Terry Jones the technical officer in charge and Eric Harris a technical officer. It was like a totalitarian regime that was controlled totally by Terry, everything was done by strict rules and set order – things I always hated. Working indoors was not really me, and repetition certainly wasn't me. Day after day bank cleaning, relay adjusting, meter testing, maintenance schedules and generally getting bored made my time here unbearable. Then there was Terry, a very professional and respected individual – who didn't like change or anything that strayed from his daily routine. We would probably label it bullying today but in those days, you just shut up and got on with it.

Terry would call tea break every day at 9.30am, after being there since 7.30am. We moved into the 'rest room' where I had made the tea and Terry had placed himself in his 'chair', nothing was going to move him for the next 30 minutes as he sat there reading the Daily Telegraph. If the telephone, any of them including the 'Special Faults' phone, rang during this sacred period it was ignored, but stupidly I would go and answer it, as I was supposed to do when not having tea. If I then came back to the rest room and told Terry he was needed I got a very sharp response! Lunchtime and the afternoon tea break were no better. Sit in his chair and you were dead, unfortunately many of the external engineers came in earlier and if they didn't know the process would sit in 'his' chair. Oh, dear!

Finally, the day came, the review by the Training Officer. Reviewing performance reports, college and course grades and deciding my future. He told me that I was going on exchange maintenance, onto being a technical officer in training – all from Stroud exchange, I went home totally distraught, no way going back there with Terry. Three years training and ending up in the worst job I could ever imagine. My father was an engineer, he did his apprenticeship at Gloster Aircraft, built planes during the war and even did part-time firefighting every night during the Blitz.

The oldest photo I possess of my father, here on the far right as an apprentice toolmaker at Gloster Aircraft Company in WW2. He is standing next to a Gloster Gladiator that they were building at the outbreak of war, he would have been about 19 at the time

When I told him he didn't mince his words, 'tell them you aren't going to do it, tell them what you want to do and, if they say no, jack the job in. There is no way they will throw away a fully trained apprentice just to satisfy themselves'. So, I did just that - and it worked!

I said I wanted to become a subscriber maintenance engineer and they grudgingly agreed, not sure what Terry thought not getting the engineer of his dreams, but I was over the moon. Six months' final training with John Melhuish and Keith Munckton at Brimscombe and I was ready to rock in the summer of 1972, just coming out of my teens. Basically Terry made my life hell, but a few years on and we were actually good colleagues, strange how things turn out eventually.

Winter 1972, fresh out of my apprenticeship and about to leave my teens, my first GPO van here at Chavenage

My first day as a relief engineer covering an area I knew very well from my apprenticeship. Maurice Screen had been temporarily promoted and moved up to a position working in the Stroud area, so I took on Nailsworth, etc. My first fault was a 'coin jam' in the AA box up on Calcot Crossroads (A46), this I coped with easily. Then the next was a 'bell not ringing' at a house in Nailsworth, a very large house. The house had a set-up with multiple phones spread around the house and even an extension bell in the garden. All the phones worked but none of them rang on an incoming call. I was starting to wish I had listened more to the trainer in my apprenticeship as I was completely baffled and didn't know what to do next.

After an hour getting nowhere, I retreated to the exchange where I met Trevor Panter, he was a relief exchange technical officer from Dursley. As luck would have it Trevor had also been subscriber maintenance engineer and was happy to help me out. "Bring your N series diagrams in and we will go through them", which threw me completely as I didn't think I had any, but looking behind the passenger seat in my van I found a box full of folders containing dozens of wiring diagrams. At this point I truly wished I had paid more attention during the last 6 months of my apprenticeship. With Trevor's advice firmly fixed in my head back I went to the house and found the broken wire that was the cause of the problem, their dog had chewed part of the telephone cable on one of the extensions – result! Not a good start to my first day though, and I had a lot more to learn over the coming months, if not years as I moved into my 20's.

This book is filled with stories from a very full 19 years of growing up, with masses of adventures along the way. As I said right at the beginning - we know how lucky children and teenagers are today but, in a village setting with no internet, no computers, no TV, no mobile phone, no expensive toys, no fast food, no electric scooters, no foreign holidays - and no central heating what did we do?

Well, now you know (but at least we had a post office and most towns had several banks, unlike today!).

My father died in 1989, my mother in 1991. I scattered their ashes at the Rover Hut where they first met that fateful day in 1937, together once more.

THE END – OR IS IT?

HOLD ON - 2019!

Early in 2019 I thought it would be interesting to track down as many of my ex-pupils from Kingscourt School and plan a reunion, roughly after 60 years. With the aid of social media and a knack for research I managed to locate many, even those no longer living in the area and one in Australia and another in Cyprus. The initial plan was to hold it in the Kings Head until I was contacted by the owner of the old school, which had been converted to a house a few decades before. He offered us his house and garden, which used to be the playground, for our get together and I accepted. In August that year twelve of us met for the first time in decades, and for me the first time back there.

The 'Tortoise stove' still there!

This was our classroom, as featured in an earlier B&W photo with Mrs. Cox – transformation!

The incredible mezzanine conversion

The original cast iron gate still looking out onto Bowl Hill, but no more tarmac playground

The playground now a beautiful garden

The pegs and the dap bags have gone but the entrance hallway remains

We had many photos and memories to share, and cakes and wine. Sadly, Jonathan Critchley died a few years ago although I did see him again after the reunion. To end on a high note though – his brother Neil married Jenny Little (Didcot) last year.

August 2019 and the reunion in the old playground, where the outside toilets used to be. L to R – Melvyn Wilkins, Neil Critchley, Jonathan Critchley, John Grange, Trevor Marks, Peter Hocking and Roger Griffin. Front row L to R – Sue Stevens, Joy Edwards, Jenny Didcot, Jenny Short and Eira Savage.

BIOGRAPHY!

I moved away from the Stroud area to the Forest of Dean in 2006. After 25 years at GPO/Post Office Telephones/BT, I had a career change in 1994 and moved into the veterinary environment. From 1994 to 2004 I was the practice manager at Clockhouse Veterinary Hospital in Wallbridge.

Following major cancer surgery in 2018 I decided to retire from my final employment at Allianz Insurance (Petplan), but I continue to work as a Trustee of our local community association. Married to Mandy I have two children from my first marriage – Amber, who lives in Vancouver and Aaron, who lives in Stroud. Mandy has a son Mitchell, who also lives in Stroud.

In 1974 I became a Chartered Freeman of the City of Gloucester, and on January 1st, 1982, I was awarded in the New Year Honours for meritorious service while serving in RAF Strike Command as a reservist.

Freeman Ceremony at the Guildhall, September 5th, 1974

THE FREEMAN'S OATH

City of Gloucester
TO WIT

YOU shall swear that you shall be a true Liegeman, and true Faith and Truth bear unto our Sovereign Lady the Queen's Majesty, her Heirs and lawful Successors, and to your power shall aid and assist the Mayor, Sheriff, and Council of this CITY OF GLOUCESTER, for the time being, and to them shall be obedient for and concerning such Things as they, or any of them, shall lawfully and reasonably will and command you to do: You shall well and truly observe, perform, fulfil, and keep all such Orders and Rules as are, and shall be, made and established by the Council of this City, for the good Government thereof, in all things to you appertaining. You shall also give, yield, and be contributory to and with the Corporation of this City so far forth as you ought, or shall be chargeable to do. And you shall not, by Colour of your Freedom, bear out, or cover under you any Foreign Person or Stranger, or their Goods and Chattels: but according to the best of your Skill, Wit, Cunning, and Power, you shall uphold and maintain all the Liberties, Franchises, good Customs, Orders and Usages of this City and Corporation. So HELP YOU GOD.

MELVYN ALBERT FRANK WILKINS, of 61, Chandos Road, Rodborough, Stroud, Telecommunications Engineer, *was Sworn a Burgess, and Freeman of the City aforesaid, the* Fifth *day of* September *in the year of our Lord One Thousand Nine Hundred and* Seventy-four.

H R T Shackleton
Chief Executive Officer.

The Freeman's Oath, signed by H R T Shackleton (CEO)

Receiving my New Year Honours citation

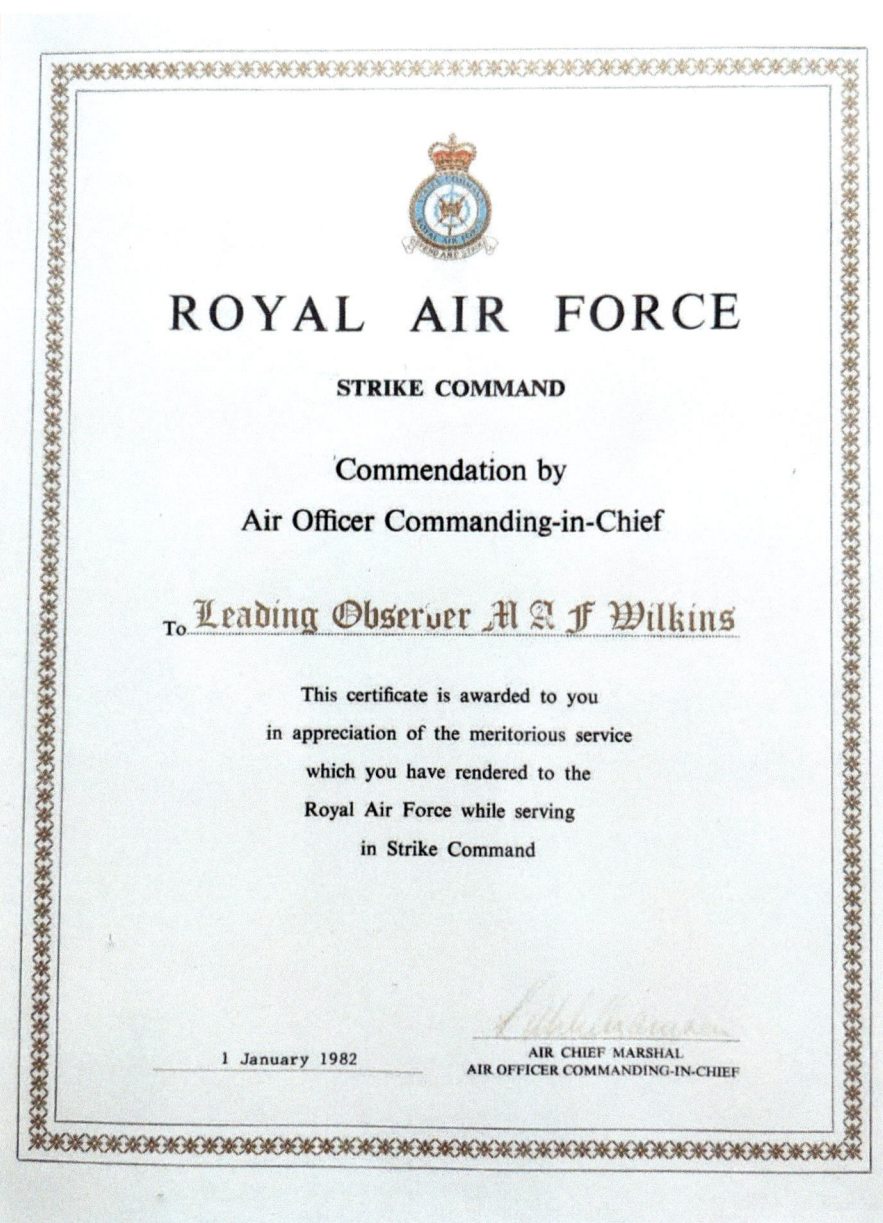

The citation from the Air Chief Marshal

I run my own Facebook page – Melvyn's Switzerland and France Photography. I also run a Facebook group – Royal Forest Classic Cars and I am honoured to be a Moderator for The Switzerland Pictures Community Facebook group with 137,000 members globally.

In 2021 I published my first book – *"SWITZERLAND. The scenery, The people, The trains – The Whole Experience. A very personal journey over 57 years"*. This was followed in 2023 by a second book – *"From Stroud Valleys to Alpine Passes"* a chronicle of the 70 years of Beavis Travel and Rover Coaches. In 2024 my third book – *"Dehydrated Chicken Supreme and other great Scouting adventures"* charted my time in the local Scout community between 1961-1987. My fourth book was published in 2025 – *"At the third stroke it will be ……."* followed my career in the GPO/Post Office Telephones/BT full of the amazing, bizarre, amusing and dangerous activities which would not exist in this modern politically correct and health and safety conscious world.

Finally, apart from Mandy, I share our home with two adorable Maine Coon cats – Rzeka and Saturn, and I share the drive with my fabulous 1980 Triumph Dolomite Sprint.

Is there still another book left in me?